Parenting With
PRAYER

Mary Ann Kuharski

Our Sunday Visitor Publishing Division
Our Sunday Visitor, Inc.
Huntington, Indiana 46750

International Standard Book Number: 0-87973-553-8
Library of Congress Catalog Card Number: 93-83241

Cover design by Rebecca J. Heaston

PRINTED IN THE UNITED STATES OF AMERICA

553

To all those who strive to raise children in faith and love;
to my earthly mother who was the first to teach me about Jesus;
and to Mary my heavenly Mother,
who answers all my pleas — always bringing me back to her Son.

TOP ROW (from left): Theresa, Tina, Tim, Chrissy and Andy, Tony, Charlie, Mary Elizabeth, Angela.

MIDDLE ROW: Kari, Michael, John, Mary Ann, Grandma D (for Delmonico, Mary Ann's mother).

ON LAPS: Joseph and Dominic.

TABLE OF CONTENTS

Allow Me to Introduce You to. . .

After twenty-three years of parenting, I'll be the first to admit I don't have all the answers.

I do know one thing: Parenting with prayer and God's grace as my strength have made my career as a "mom to many" easier and a whole lot more fun. I'm still learning to take myself less seriously and God more seriously, to rely on him and not on me.

The way I see it, my kids (like all other children) were created by God and are merely "on loan" to us. It's our job to figure out the best way to get them back where they belong — with him in heaven.

As for the following material, I am sure there are many good books on parenting. There are even more good books — beginning with *the* Good Book — on prayer. What I've attempted to do in these few pages is offer a mom's eye view of the Catholic faith as applied to the vocation of parenthood — and *vocation* it most assuredly is. To help those who have this time-consuming but wonderful vocation, I've included some of our family's favorite prayers, which have been "tried and tested," used and reused.

The latest polls report that the majority of American couples average 2.3 children per family. Aren't you dying to know what those .3 kids look like? Where are they and what happened to their other parts? That's what I want to know. Let me assure you that all of our kids, the adopteds and the "tummies," are each and every one a hundred-percent child. Some are now grown, a few more are on their way, and the rest are in the "molding and shaping" process.

John and I didn't purposely set out to challenge the "norm" or defy the trends, but I must say I'll bet the life we've had with our colorful crew (couldn't resist the pun) of thirteen, is a lot more exciting than those who insisted (some have no choice) on holding the line at the socially acceptable — but boring — 2.3.

All of our thirteen children — seven of whom came by "tummy" (as the kids say) and six by "airport" (or adoption)

— have given John and me an intangible gift that can't be bought and can't be stolen. They've broadened our horizons, stretched our vision, and continually keep us wondering, "What do couples do *without* chaos, commotion, and the cuddles that can only come with kids?"

We quickly learned that each child is *unique* — a constellation, a revelation, a mystery, and a blessing. Though not without "flaw," they — by their mere presence — brought us closer to God, closer to each other, and more in love with everything and everyone.

Allow me to introduce them to you (by the way, their ages are as of September, 1993):

Christine, twenty-five [tummy] ♥ Chrissy is the sweet, good-natured, do-for-others personality that got the show on the road and made us want more. (Little did we dream!) I think this kid became a second mother and "big sister" at birth and, in spite of her age and the changes in her life, still relishes her role as the "oldest." It is Chrissy that the others look to as their counselor, consoler, and, most of all, cheerleader. When she was at home and head of the herd, she was the backyard organizer, the parade and picnic planner, and the "won't this be fun?" leader.

Family is everything to Chrissy, and where some could have resented a childhood of "close quarters" and constant sharing, Chrissy displayed an almost unlimited ability to give and to share. And now that's she's grown, she is not only helpful and supportive to me and to her brothers and sisters, she's especially attentive to her grandparents: running their errands, doing their housecleaning, and looking after their needs.

From head to toe, Chrissy spells "l-o-v-e." It's no wonder she's the darling of the family.

And now she's grown and doing what she loves best: teaching and inspiring a roomful of rambunctious third graders at St. Charles Borromeo Catholic School. She refers to them as "her kids" and delights in each one.

When Chrissy chose a husband, she made sure he was "the kind of guy who loves my family, too." And who is this great guy? His name is Andy Klaesges and he joined our family in August, 1990, blending in with our crew as if he'd always belonged.

An electrician by trade, Andy is an all-around handyman. I don't think there's anything he *can't* do. When Chrissy and Andy moved into their first "starter" home, Andy immediately began painting, papering, plumbing, rewiring, and reinsulating. Chrissy confides, "It's scary coming in the door at night. I never know what Andy's going to tackle next." His plans to "raise the roof," add another room, rebuild the garage, and rip out the old furnace he's nicknamed "The Octopus" are just some of his latest "things to do." That is, if he can find the time.

One of Andy's best qualities is his eagerness to pitch in and share his skill and talent. Whether they're projects for church, family, or friends, Andy's there to help, and he does a first-rate job every time! Since Andy moved into our hearts, the wiring, lamps, lighting, and other Mr. Fixit repairs in our home have never looked better!

A rich mixture of simplicity, he says it like he sees it: with no fancy airs or pretenses. Give him a hammer, a home-cooked meal, a "beater" truck that runs, and a life dictated by common sense, faith, and family, and Andy's happy. So are we, to have such a blessing in our lives.

Chrissy and Andy live about a mile away and are often with us for Sunday dinners or weekends at Grandma K's two-bedroom cabin enjoying the challenge of making do with cots and tents. When it comes time for family vacations, guess whose little red Pontiac Sunbird caravans with us? (Incidentally, if you haven't already guessed, Grandma K — God rest her soul — was my husband's mother. She died in 1989.)

And the best bonus of all? Chrissy and Andy are soon to be parents, making us grandparents for the first time. God is so good!

Tim, twenty-three [tummy] ♥ Tall, blonde, and handsome, Tim is a copy of his Polish dad in looks and shyness. Underneath that "still water," however, runs a river that can rush and rage when stirred, much like his Italian mother. I tell him, "You may look Polish, but there's an Italian in there somewhere!"

Tim is thoughtful, warm, sweet, and really fun to have around. His naturally quiet manner is an inviting respite, especially when some of my more "active" attention-getters are doing their level best to give their mother high blood pressure.

Tim knows a bit about mischievousness himself and really was the first one who dared march to a different tune. None of us will ever forget the Christmas that Tim, then five, got up in the middle of the night and unwrapped all the gifts that were under the tree and put them away, then ate all the candy stuffed in the once-hung stockings and was back in bed before the rest of us woke up to discover what appeared to be a ransacking or robbery! And yes, he did get a spanking.

It was this child who taught me how to relax, to rethink my priorities about such things as handprints on tables and mischief over perfectionism.

I'll admit we had a few battles when he was a teen and living at home. He bristled at our strict curfew rules and Mom's "archaic" views. And now that he's working (a CPA like his father) and living on his own, it's Tim who takes me to lunch on occasion and, after listening to the latest Kuharski capers, will smile broadly, pat me on the arm, and say, "Stick to your guns, Mom; you know you're right!" Now, that's maturity!

No one else can flash you a smile or reach down (we're talking six-foot-plus here) for a hug that will curl your socks and steal your heart. He's a luv!

Charlie, twenty-three [adopted] ♥ Of black/Cambodian parents, Charlie arrived at age five and a half from an orphanage in Saigon. His memory of those early years and a family destroyed by the Vietnam war left an emotional scar that soon faded as he embraced us and the ready-made family who wanted only to love him.

Charlie is our philosopher. He loves to chew on an issue, exhaust the concepts, and rehash the conclusions. He's more interested in standing for principle and truth than he is in popularity or peace at any price. While some in today's world boast of caring for the environment or the non-threatening issues of the age, Charlie stands out. He's not afraid to wear a pro-life T-shirt on a secular campus (I suspect he rather enjoys the challenge), or to question the status quo if he believes it is not right.

Charlie had his taste of the "other" world, living in a frat house and experiencing the freedom of college life. After two years of a rather "unstructured" existence, he opted to return to a more disciplined environment — not home but the United States Air Force. Our son Tony told him he was smart: "The Air Force has got to be easier on ya than living at home with Mom's rules!"

Today Charlie is diligently working to carry a full load of college credits toward an engineering degree while he's on active duty with the Air Force. Much to his mother's surprise (and delight!), Charlie has become a youth group leader at the church near his base. In fact, he recently spent his military leave in Denver to see the Holy Father, Pope John Paul II, at the World Youth Rally.

Everyone enjoys being with Charlie. He's a people lover with a personality that is genuine, warm, and outgoing. And when this guy gives you a hug, every rib in your "cage" knows you've been loved!

Tina, twenty-two [adopted] ♥ As our first adopted child, Tina, a Filipino, arrived when she was eighteen months old. She was like a rosebud, so "tight and closed" to our affection the first few years. In fact, biting, spitting, and throwing food were more her forte than anything else. As time passed, our "Rosebud" opened and displayed a grace, trust, and love more beautiful than we ever imagined.

Presently in her last year of college, she is paying (or borrowing) her way toward a much-desired nursing degree. She plans a career working with the elderly, and if her part-time skill is any hint of the future, the patients in her charge will be cuddled, catered to, and cared for like never before. At home or on the job, Tina is our Florence Nightingale. Her heart bleeds at the mere whisper of the word "suffer."

Tina, like her sister Chrissy, is cause-oriented. One day she called home to say she "slept in a cardboard box to show compassion for the homeless." Never mind the danger, the thirty-degree temperature, or the twenty-six inches of snow on the ground! When I expressed my concern, she replied over the phone, "Oh, mom, relax, will ya? We sat up and listened to the radio and talked all night." As if a portable radio and talking to a girlfriend made it warm and safe!

She spent one winter break, not "beaching" in Florida like most kids her age, but washing walls for the homeless and marching in a peace rally. Last year the poor in Mexico got her free weeks. We've tried telling her about our walls that need scrubbing, and the little Mexican at our house, but — according to her — she's not into "domestic" issues.

Our younger girls look to Tina as the sister of the world who knows the most about fashion and hairstyling, of what's "in" and what's not! When she comes home, whether it's for weekends, holidays, or her summer R 'n' R, the whole house livens up! And when she's not around, I freely admit that perhaps I, more than anyone, miss the bubbly enthusiasm, warmth, and love that only Tina can add to a dinner table!

Anthony, twenty [adopted] ♥ A Vietnamese, Tony was our "miracle baby" who arrived via an emergency medical visa, which was stamped "child will not survive orphanage life." Born in an intensive care nursery/orphanage, when he arrived at two months of age he weighed a scant five pounds and was diagnosed with starvation diarrhea, dehydration, and malnutrition.

While his first few months were admittedly "touch and go," Tony has always seemed to defy the odds. With Tony came warnings of hearing loss, unknown medical risks, and mental limitations. Not so. Some may say it was time, nutrition, and lots of hands-on love. I know it was mostly prayer.

Tony's slow and precarious beginning gave way to a youngster with energy, electricity, and enthusiasm unmatched! Nowadays such a child would be called "hyperactive." The kids used to call him "Motor Mouth." I called him my "creative genius," and while he did have his difficulties adapting to school and discipline, he is already doing good things — for himself and for others.

He recently traded in his college texts for a four-year stint with the United States Army. He called home from Berlin (collect — naturally!) the other day, asking for prayers: "I figure I need all the help I can get. We're being shipped to Bosnia." When I asked if he was wearing a scapular for protection, he replied, "I even put up a crucifix in my room and my little statue of St. Anthony. My agnostic roommate complained, but I told him, 'Half the room belongs to me.'" That's Tony!

He is not only bright and creative, he's also sensitive, fun, and always able to lighten up any place or situation with his marvelous humor and wit. The best word to describe Tony is *spark*! And we all know there would be no fire, no love, and no zest in life without a spark! I hope he never changes.

Vincent, twenty-two [adopted] ♥ Arriving from Calcutta, Vincent — of East Indian ancestry — was estimated to be about nine, ten, or "older" in age. Unbeknownst to us, most of his life had been spent "on the streets," and we soon realized that while his bodily frame was that of a child, he had seen and experienced more deprivation and abuse than most grown men could handle.

Vincent had some serious physical handicaps, including a cleft palate, hearing loss in both ears (requiring aids), and cerebral palsy in his legs. His greatest obstacle, however, was emotional. He was a child who had suffered a lifetime of neglect, abandonment, and serious abuse, and we heartbreakingly learned he could not accept what he considered to be the smothering and stifling commitment of family life.

With Vincent, we learned the real meaning of unconditional love, as well as the most difficult lesson of all — that some handicaps simply cannot be overcome, once a youngster's childhood has been filled with hurt and hostility. After a five-year struggle — involving hospitalizations, treatment centers, and ongoing psychological therapy — Vincent, at sixteen, chose to live in a supervised foster arrangement. His departure and separation from the family was a loss that affected us profoundly.

Theresa, nineteen [adopted] ♥ Theresa, of black and Caucasian parents, came to us at the age of two and a half. She was well loved and cared for by a foster family, yet her adoption was held up in part because of a Minnesota state law mandating that mixed and minority adoptable children be placed only with "matching" parents. The addition of Charlie to our family changed our status from "white" to minority, thus allowing us to adopt Theresa.

In my book, these kinds of silly laws made by adults at the expense of children are a crime. It makes little sense to me that we could easily adopt a child of any race — black included — from other parts of the globe, and yet kids right in our own state *wait* because someone decided they will be deprived of their cultural heritage and pride if they're allowed to be adopted by white couples. Never mind that there is a shortage of minority adoptive couples. Whatever became of "adoption in the best interest of the child"? Excuse my "soapbox," but I feel better now!

Theresa was a preemie who also had a fragile beginning. Fortunately for her, she was well cared for by physicians at the Mayo Clinic in Rochester, Minnesota, where she was diagnosed as having mental limitations and a hereditary or congenital problem. In a nutshell, we needed her and she needed us!

Surpassing all expectations, and thanks to a wonderful assortment of special-education instructors, Theresa recently graduated from high school.

Her kitchen talents and previous part-time experience at McDonald's recently landed her a job at a local nursing home where she eventually hopes to try her skill in areas other than dishes, food, and cleanup.

When she's not listening to her radio, always singing along in her melodious voice, she's deep in study — alternating between the J. C. Penney catalogue and daily ads. (Dreaming never hurts!)

Working with Theresa has taught me patience and chipped away at my imperfections. She taught us to take the world less seriously and helped us appreciate the meaning of the word "progress."

Theresa is going to hold her own someday. There's a niche just for her. When she gets there, John and I will be the ones with the soppy "we knew you could do it, kid" grins across our faces.

There isn't anyone more eager to please than Theresa.

She's a bundle of kindness and warmth in our lives and a sheer blessing to us.

Mary Elizabeth, fifteen [tummy] ♥ In spite of her desire to change her name to "just plain Mary," she is and will always be our Mary Elizabeth. This "Dimpled Darling Number One," as Grandma D nicknamed her, was number seven and the "surprise" that started us on our second family. (By the way, Grandma D, as pointed out in the family photo on page 4, is my mom.)

Mary Elizabeth arrived the year I finally got all the kids (then totaling six) in school and had selfishly plotted to "do my thing." "No more kids," I resolved. But God knew better. Thank heavens he did! Mary made us feel young again. Who could get too absorbed in adolescent or teen trials with a baby in the house! The whole family seemed to liven up with "little Mare-Mare," as the older kids called her.

Mary is quiet, shy, thoughtful, and sweet. Her easy-natured, never-demanding, yet "persistent as a dog on a pants leg" style, tends to win over any but the most hardened of hearts. Why else would any mother in her right mind say "yes" to a pet rat?

Affectionately nicknamed the "Sponge," Mary Elizabeth is the household know-it-all and gossip. She says little, yet *nothing* gets past her as far as who's doing what and who isn't supposed to know about it!

Mary Elizabeth is selfless, kind, and considerate — toward *everyone*. Although she's not known for her tidiness, she's been a constant support and helper around the house, without being asked or told.

You'll never catch Mary being gushy or overly demonstrative. "Cool as a cucumber" is more her style. Yet when I need help or there's trouble in the air, Mary Elizabeth is there.

For someone born with a smile, a twinkle in her eye, and a quiet flow of love and warmth, no one can hold a candle to Mary Elizabeth! Little wonder then that after her unplanned arrival, we had a change of heart and begged God for more.

Angela, thirteen [tummy] ♥ Give the kid an audience or a telephone and she can charm just about anybody. If there's an event or a party happening somewhere, Angela knows about it. And wants to go, of course! She's on the phone, or with a friend, or running from one event to another and asking for permission to do even more in between. She's exhausting!

In the course of her short history, she's been into volleyball, basketball, ballet, tap dance, piano, and most recently flute, each one giving her and her "ham" sister, Kari, an opportunity to perform.

When the school has a fund-raiser, it's Angie who sneaks my address book and isn't the least bit shy about calling all of *my* friends and acquaintances to hit them up for a donation. She did so well one year, she even begged on behalf of Kari and her little brothers.

Angie is loving, caring, and warm, yet has little time for chores or housework: "It's so boring!" she'll say. She's a "people person" literally bubbling with ideas and enthusiasm. And when she's telling a story, her eyes widen, her face lights up, and her body exudes more excitement and energy than any marching band.

To Angie "all the world's a stage," and if you're looking for one of the most creative, imaginative, energetic minds in our clan, latch on to Angie. It's like riding a star!

Karen (Kari), eleven [tummy] ♥ Kari and Angie are so close that some suspect they're "joined at the hip." In fact, one year their Christmas wish list asked for "clothes so we can be twins."

Angie thinks of it and Kari carries it out! Kari is our chatterbox and talker, the third of our "dimpled darlings" to come along.

Once shy and coquettish, Kari is about as determined as a runaway steamroller when she has something on her mind. She and Angie are roommates, which means there is always a new creation or caper in the wings. At present, their world includes two pet rabbits, the offspring of the one they had bred. (It beats white rats!)

Kari makes up in humor and wit what Angie offers in imagination and vision. She's a reader, an observer, and a mimic, occasionally bringing us all to tears of laughter with her imitations of high society or worse yet — us. The other kids claim she has my quirks and mannerisms down to such a science that, one evening when I was out, she sat in my chair at dinner and did a perfect rendition of "Mom." Hmmm.

Both a couple of clowns, Angie and Kari are now the ones to entertain and create the fun for their younger brothers, who hang on to their every idea!

For a happy, sweet-natured, and always-time-for-a-hug personality, Kari can't be beat!

Michael, nine [tummy] ♥ Michael takes after his Grandpa Kuharski in looks, stature, and shyness. He loves to remind us that he is "either the tallest or almost the tallest" in his fourth-grade class.

Michael is shy, gentle, kind, and just naturally considerate unless he's being taunted beyond even "water torture" standards by his kid brother Dominic.

Michael's favorite pastime is sports, with a special interest in baseball. His collection of baseball cards has taken over a small suitcase, a couple of scrapbooks, and two shoe boxes. All I keep asking is, "Who ate all that gum?" No one's talking, but for some reason, Dominic appears happier than Michael!

Michael is my early-morning alarm system. I know my day is about to begin when he either comes upstairs for a "minute to cuddle" or I hear the front door unlatch as he goes outside to get the sports section of the daily paper "to see how the Twins did."

Michael loves to eat (like his dad and Grandpa K), and we rarely finish a meal before he's asking, "Now what's for dessert?"

One of his most cherished moments was serving as ring bearer for his sister Chrissy and Andy's wedding. (Chrissy also happens to be Michael's godmother.) His quiet shyness didn't hold him back one bit. He, like some of the other hams around here, seemed to relish the spotlight.

Michael's road to tolerance, if not sainthood, may begin by his survival of the taunts of younger brother Dominic.

For a loving, wrap-around-your-heart squeeze, Michael just waits to be invited!

Dominic, seven [adopted] ♥ Dominic, who is lovingly referred to as our "Mexican tornado," is like an electrical current. From the moment our Mexican/American's eyes open in the morning, he's up, he's active, and he's charged for action!

He has dark-brown soulful eyes and an impish grin that has saved his hide from many a thrashing. In fact, there are times I'm tempted to take his temperature if he's *not* into something awful!

In his younger years, he singlehandedly peeled the wallpaper off one bedroom wall and left his "free form" art (pen, pencil, crayon, markers, gum!) in several rooms throughout the house. Maybe he's going to be a famous interior decorator or artist. I have a feeling he's also going to have more experience than most at wall washing and reparation!

Dommie is another of those "hyperactive" challenges who does well when he's kept very busy and warmly encouraged. If left up to him, he could easily become addicted to gadgets, electronics, TV, and video games. This is one "mean" mom, however, who pushes outdoor play and physical exercise, carefully controlling the very kind of "brain drains" he finds so alluring.

He loves to help out in the kitchen, works very hard to please, and — underneath all the mischief-making energy — craves tenderness and love: ingredients we thrive on dishing out!

Joseph, five [tummy] ♥ God's "afterthought" is our late-in-life, "once more for old times' sake" surprise, and if I say he is the apple of his dad's eye and sheer joy to this over-forty mom, it would be putting it mildly!

Joseph, who resembles big sister Chrissy, is a lover and a nonstop talker. From morning till night he's talking, and if I dare to respond with a shrug or a sigh, he taps me and demands, "Don't say 'ah huh.' Talk, Mama."

Following in Michael and Dominic's footsteps he went through all the normal stages — smudging walls, plugging toilets, smearing windows, and drinking the Kuharski kids' version of imported Perrier: toilet water!

He's spoiled rotten, and it's all the other kids' fault. They treat him like such a baby! The entire family seems to revolve around "little Joe" and he around them! Only three feet plus, he includes himself in every conversation and family event. Whether he "shoots hoops" like one of the guys with the big kids, follows Angie and Kari on their paper route chattering all the way, or just tagging along "with the gang," Joseph assumes we couldn't get along without him! And he's right! He's pure gift and a blessing to our lives!

When I was young and unmarried, I once dreamed of traveling around the globe. But God did me one better. He brought the world to me, and with it came love with an international flavor that only God could have designed. Now that's what I call "family planning"!

Johnny ♥ None of this would have happened — no child, no dream, no commitment, and no vision — without my soulmate, lover, friend, and husband, John.

Though we are similar in faith and fundamental beliefs, we are as different as night and day. I am the high-strung Italian with a type A personality. John is my mild-mannered logician who slows me down, makes me consider all aspects (I hate details), and persuades me to weigh all consequences. Yuk! I like to just rush in and do whatever needs to be done. I'll worry about the "ifs" later.

My full-blooded Polish husband is one of the kindest, most considerate men I know. I would never have dared, nor desired, to take on the parenting of thirteen children, were it not for the partnership, the fun, the humor, the "sleeves-rolled-up help," and the love of my Johnny.

Some men want lots of kids. They seem to collect them like marks on a holster, but they leave the work and the worry to their wives. Not Johnny. Our venture began with a commitment and love for each other that ultimately flowed to our young. We are God's blending, and I praise the Lord for Johnny, my stabilizer and strength, who helped make marriage and parenting full of more love and surprises than I'd ever imagined possible.

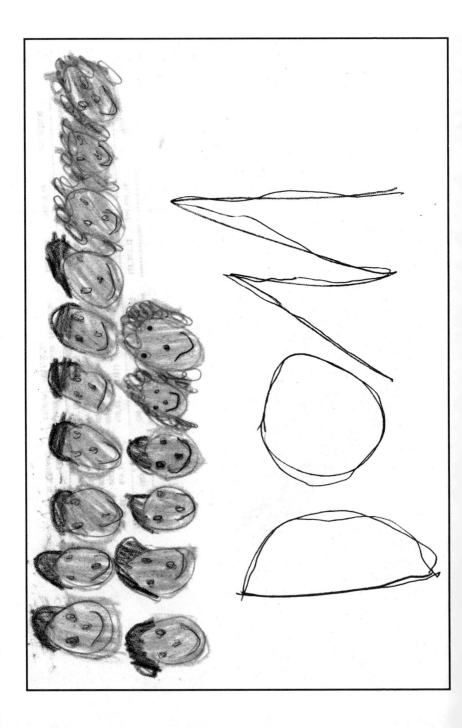

1

❦

'Don't You Believe in Family Planning?'

Ask any parents today — especially those daring to have more than the socially "correct" *two* — if they've ever encountered hostility, and chances are you'll get more than an earful.

"We weren't prepared for the negative reaction and intimidation," one young couple of three small preschoolers recalled. "What hurt the most were the remarks made by the very people we thought would be supportive — our own family and friends," confided the wife.

Listen in during any chat session at a "Mom's Morning Out" coffee hour at church and you'll hear the same: Christian couples wishing to have more than the socially "correct" two are challenged and chided as never before.

Part of the problem is a "me-first" culture that projects the notion that having children will drain and deprive you. Sometimes it does. But most of us still believe it's worth every ounce of effort. More than that, as people of faith we believe that children are a gift from a loving God, to be celebrated and embraced.

The best response we can offer, then, is encouragement and love. After all, if the Christian community does not reach out in support, who will? Perhaps if we'd take the time to congratulate a couple with a newly announced pregnancy, offer food or a baked dish to a young mother, or just let parents (or parents-to-be) know by a card or a squeeze that we share in their joy, the positives would eliminate the negatives.

"I hope you're not going to give up that wonderful career," one young friend was told after announcing her pregnancy. Another was warned, "Don't let yourself get stuck in a rut by being away from the *real* world for too long."

And then there are those who treat pregnancy like a condition or disease: "You young people are luckier than we were. You can take something to prevent it."

One of my college-age daughters once called home and asked, "Did you ever resent setting aside your career just to stay home and take care of us kids?" "What career was that?" I replied. "You mean that piddling little job I once had of pushing papers? I know it looks like all I do around here is wipe bottoms and noses. But believe me, what I'm doing is far more important. I'm raising tomorrow's future." And I am.

I must admit that as a "seasoned" mom of many, there are times when even I've been caught off guard by some of the queries posed. Normally, I'm polite. I understand that initial reaction: *"Thirteen* children, I can't imagine it!" I once couldn't either!

I confess there's a devilish side of me that wishes I could offer a teasing response. To the ones who ask, "How did that happen?" I'd like to say, "You mean you don't know?" And to those who ask, "Do you work besides?" I'd reply, "I used to. But now I just stay home and have babies."

Apparently some who learn of our family size for the first time automatically conjure up the fairy-tale image of "the old woman in the shoe who had so many children — she didn't know what to do." The next question I usually get is, "How big is your house?" or more specifically, "How many bedrooms do you have?" It's not where they sleep that's the problem. It's feeding them and finding them underwear and matching socks that's driving me nuts.

To those who ask, "They can't all be yours, can they?" I'd like to respond, "That's what I keep saying. But they keep showing up for supper and throwing their dirty clothes down the laundry chute."

Then there are those visionaries who get down to the *real* problem with housing thirteen children: "You must have a lot of bathrooms?" As if everyone gets the urge at the same time. Actually most parents quickly realize that where there's more than four in a household, there are *never* enough bathrooms!

"I send the real fidgety ones who look like they can't hold

it another minute over to the neighbors," I've teasingly told a few.

"They don't all live at home, do they?" is by far the most common question I get. As if *no* house could hold thirteen growing kids. I'm always tempted to tell people, "Well, actually until we get a couple more bunk beds, we've put a few in cold storage in the freezer and a couple in the trunk of the car." But that wouldn't be polite and may cause a few raised eyebrows!

I'm beginning to understand my grandmother's response to people who asked her how she managed with eight. She would simply reply: "I expect they were outside a lot." The gutsy lady left inquirers with the notion that after birthing her kids she just let them wander out the back door to fend for themselves, much like a stray dog or cat. Sure doesn't explain how they all turned into such fine adults.

And then we have the prophets of poverty who write articles warning that it "will cost the average couple $100,000 to raise *just one child* to age eighteen." It must drive 'em crazy to hear of couples like us who are raising a baker's dozen or more on *one income*!

My all-time favorite is, "You *must* have help." Well, need I say that if there's anyone who could have used "help," it's gotta be me? But it's a little late for that now.

I don't mean to lecture, but aren't we a bunch of wimps and whiners? I mean we've got to be living in the softest and cushiest of ages with our automatic *everything* — from washers and dryers to dishwashers and microwaves — as well as disposables and every other available convenience at our fingertips. Yet we've been led to believe that parenting more than one child virtually can't be done without "help."

Compared to our grandparents who raised large families and struggled through economic disasters, wars, depression, and unemployment (and considered even one indoor bathroom a convenience), we've got it made!

Of course, there are a certain number of people who expect us "moms of more than the acceptable two" to be weary and worn out. Some days we are. Our reward comes, however, in those hugs, laughs, and expressions of love the outside world cannot experience or comprehend.

"You're John Kuharski's wife? You're not at all what I pictured. You're actually pretty," one poor woman blurted out at a large social gathering before she could stop herself. Hmmm. The most I could do was smile.

By the way, a new phrase is emerging. Coined by the antifamily "no kids for us" promoters, it's called "child-free." One political writer woefully wrote that even in this "progressive age" the thought of a married couple purposely choosing *not to have children* is still seen as a negative. (Tsk-tsk.)

In order to change that, she suggests they adopt the theme "child-free" — kind of like the notion of cling-free, smoke-free, caffeine-free, or whatever's-not-good-for-you-free — forcefully letting us all know they have chosen to remain childless.

It's sad enough there are organizations like Planned Parenthood (full name: Planned Parenthood Federation of America) that feed off the taxpaying public and use their propaganda, pressure, and prejudice to convince the American people to limit the size of their family (if they must have children at all) to no more than two. But that's not enough. Some are determined to persuade us that sea porpoises, snail darters, forests, land, water, and ozone layers will only survive and prosper if we become extinct. We're to believe that "non-parenting" — another of those phrases — is economical, ecological, and certainly more ethical.

It's no coincidence that along with a radical feminist (antifamily) movement and legalized abortion came groups such as the National Organization of Non-Parents (NON) and Childless by Choice. Even some environmental extremists have gotten into the act by touting bumper stickers and slogans suggesting that "one child or none" is kinder to "mother earth." Those desiring more, often find themselves having to apologize for their lack of "planning."

I remember the time I was confronted as I waited in a checkout line at a supermarket. A woman walked over to me after noticing my obvious pregnant shape and the four little ones surrounding me, and asked, "Don't you feel any sense of obligation? Don't you care at all about others?"

"Sure I do," I told her. "You should see how many more

there are at home!" (I couldn't resist.) What a twist. I thought that's what pregnancy and parenting were all about — "caring for others."

Thankfully, and in spite of the naysayers and propagandists, there will always be those who disregard the doomsayers and have babies. In fact, millions of us consider parenting a vocation from God.

By the way, I must mention that while the "child-free" have to pay to have their furniture distressed, mine is done at no cost. With love and years of handling. Yes, the "child-free" can look forward to winters in warmth, cruises on luxury liners, controlled quiet, uninterrupted careers, programmed aging, and relentless routines.

Not for us. Many of us moms, with our husbands' sacrifice and support, willingly forgo that "climb to the corporate top" in order to climb the nursery-room stairs. We prefer the unknown, the unexpected, and the unpredictable. Show us a houseful of kids and we see creativity in progress.

To those who know no bounds and ask, "Don't you believe in family planning?" let's reassure them that all our kids are *planned, perfect, and spaced*. By God.

2

🌿

Believe It or Not, Parents Are Missionaries

Our mailman calls us "the United Nations," the school registrar calls us a "headache," and the people at church call us a "procession."

Mothering a pack of kids — two of whom are Asian, one black/Cambodian, one black/Caucasian, one East Indian, one Mexican/American, and seven who look Kuharski Polish — has brought its own share of challenges. But then so has being married.

John (my full-blooded Polish husband) and I are quite the contrast. While he's the quiet introvert and just naturally laid back, I'm the Italian extrovert who thrives on excitement and "living on the edge." He likes things to be well planned, programmed, and punctual. I don't. I'm for adventure, the unknown, squeezing in just "one more thing," and lots of "surprises."

Even our parenting techniques are different. He's mild, mellow, and patience personified, unless the kids disturb something of *his* and, then, beware of an eruption! I'm the dominant, domineering, demanding one with a hot temper and short fuse. Outside of that, I'm a pushover!

Our courtship began with friendship first. Love later. While our nationalities, personalities, and experiences were vastly different, our faith and fundamental values were the same. I've come to realize that is the key to a vibrant, happy marriage.

We've had as much excitement getting to know each other and smoothing out each other's feathers as we have in adding each new "personality" to our nest. In that regard, let me assure you that not only do our kids *look* different, they *act* different. Each is a unique character — in more ways than one. No two personalities are alike, and if "variety is the spice of life," then we've been blessed with the most incredibly rich menu of humanity any mother and father could ever wish for.

And it all happened because the "fear" of adding another just wasn't enough to stop us.

Our kids see each other in honest-yet-critical eyes. Here, in capsule form, is how they describe one another:

♥ **Chrissy:** "Our second Mom. She loves us, but she'll tell on us." Married to Andy, who is "Thrifty but nifty!" "As good as a brother!"

♥ **Timmy:** "Looks Polish, acts Italian!" "Hothead!"

♥ **Charlie:** "The philosopher." "He wants to analyze everything!"

♥ **Tina:** "So much fun — even if she's bossy!"

♥ **Vincent:** "How come he left so quick?" (Referring to his decision to live in a supervised foster arrangement.)

♥ **Tony:** "Mr. Cool." "He even walks bigtime!"

♥ **Theresa:** "Is there anyone who loves fashion more than her?"

♥ **Mary Elizabeth:** "The eyes and ears of the family." "She knows too much!"

♥ **Angela:** "All the world's a stage!" "Always trying to sneak out of the work at home!"

♥ **Kari:** "Looks are deceiving." "About as shy as a Spanish bull."

♥ **Michael:** "Timid, sweet, and persistent." "A walking 'Who's Who' on baseball heroes."

♥ **Dominic:** "If he's not 'hyper,' no one is." "Sleeps with his eyes open."

♥ **Joseph:** "Mom and Dad's bonus!" "He gets by with everything!"

Kids have a wonderful way of not noticing color or differences. They're more impressed with whether or not someone is kind or nice.

When we first moved to our big yellow house on Pahl Avenue, Tina (then six) came rushing in the door and announced, "Guess what? There's a family down the block that has *eight* kids" — two more than ours at the time — "and they all *look* alike!"

We adults can get so hung up on race and color where little children rarely notice. I remember the time Chrissy came home from school and begged to take her new brother, Tony, to kindergarten for "Show and Tell."

"Why do you want to show Tony off? Is it because he came to our family all the way from Vietnam?" I asked.

"Veetnum? I don't know 'bout that," Chrissy replied. "I just wanted to bring Tony 'cuz he's my brudder and he's so cute. Besides yesterday Melissa brought her cat and I figure if she can do that I can bring my new brudder." Obviously, baby Tony did not make it to "Show and Tell."

I remember the day our Kari first discovered that some of her brothers and sisters were not the same color. We were all eating around our picniclike kitchen table when Kari looked up from her plate across the table at Charlie and said, "Gosh. Didja guys ever notice that Chawee has a reewee bwack face?" It took five years for her to realize the difference in skin color!

Kari, by the way, is the same one who was so sure that she was one of the "airport" kids (adopteds) that she thought I was teasing when I insisted, "No, indeed. You came from Mom's tummy." (John thinks I need to spend more time teaching our own kids about sex education rather than "running around as a volunteer for the pro-life movement teaching sex education to *other* people's kids.")

There was more than one occasion when I was pregnant and one of my little ones asked, "Will this one be brown or white?" I always get a kick out of those kinds of questions unless I'm caught off guard and unprepared. Like when I'm standing in a crowded checkout lane with about six kids under foot and John's nowhere in sight. People look at my white, black, and Asian tribe, and then at me and my obviously "expecting" condition, and all but gasp. I bet they think I'm a frisky little number!

Having a mixed-racial family has not gone unnoticed — in our extended family and community. We've been gushed over and invited to events as if we were the "token blacks"; and we've been shunned and slighted for one reason and one reason only: It's spelled "skin."

I remember the time my two boys Tim and Charlie (both about ten at the time) came home crying because some older boys chased them home throwing rocks and sticks at them. After they calmed down a bit, I asked them how it all started, and Charlie began to cry again, sniffling, "They called me a name that hurt my heart." When I asked what the name was, he replied, "Nigger."

I pulled my sobbing dark-skinned son to me and held him close. As I turned around, Tim, Charlie's fair-complexioned kin, tears streaming down his cheeks, dejectedly reported, "Well, they called me 'fart-face' and I think that's just about as bad."

I hugged Tim, too, saying, "I think you're right about that. I wouldn't want to be called either one."

What *was* beautiful was Tim's obvious affection and empathy for his brother Charlie. He not only stayed by his side during the attack, his sense of kinship easily extended to the hatred and discrimination. If Charlie was hurt, Tim was, too.

Guess who was the one at dinnertime that evening to whisper an extra prayer for "those boys who don't know any better"? Yup. Charlie. I think he taught us all a lesson in forgiveness.

In all sincerity, the discrimination that hurt the worst over the years — and took the most amount of prayer and grace to accept — was that which came from family members or so-called friends. All of it, we believe, has made us stronger, better, more committed, and more forgiving.

There's a kind of kindred spirit that has grown along with our family. We may look different, and our bloodlines may be different. But a mysterious and marvelous Creator has sewn our hearts and lives together with grace and love. Isn't God good?

Frankly, the only thing I'm sure of after parenting thirteen children — the "successful" part still remains in question — is my need for faith and God. If I could offer any advice to young parents just starting out, I think I would boil it down to four things:

1 • PARENTS ARE THE FIRST MISSIONARIES TO THEIR CHILDREN. This wonderful message was repeated often by my pastor, Father Francis Kittock. It became a special source of encouragement and support to John and me, who are still "in the midst of the mess."

Quite often we parents fail to recognize that, more than anyone else, we are the first and best teachers and examples to our young.

A young mother called one day, terribly upset to learn about the "values-free" sex education and secular humanism found in her son's junior high school. Like millions of other good Christian parents, she worried about the influence and effects of such programs. Father Kittock's words shed light on the problem: "Parents hold the truth. You have the Holy Spirit to help to instill sound values and knowledge in your young." Eat your heart out, secular humanists!

In addition, here are some facts we should keep in mind: There are six hours in a school day, 180 days in the school year, which totals 1,080 hours that the child is in school. Yet there are 8,760 hours in the year, which means our children are home for 7,680 hours. In addition, children are with their parents some 40,000 hours before a teacher ever gets them. The earliest years from birth to age five are the most impressionable and formative. In essence, we have the greatest opportunity to mold our young. We also have the greatest responsibility.

We moms and dads can't be intimidated by the world around us. We must never be made to compete and/or conform, even if it's to the thinking of the latest child psychologists — some of whom wouldn't know parenting "firsthand" if it hit them in the face.

Personally speaking, my mothering improved along with my self-confidence when I began to ignore the well-meaning advisers and "experts" and relied on prayer and the *maternal* common sense and good judgment that God gave me.

Of course, this means that we ignore the occasions when we're "x-rayed" by our own children. It won't matter then if "everyone else gets to," or if "we're the only ones who don't have it," etc.

The adolescent and teen years presented the most "interesting" and challenging encounters with our young. Simple curfews and standard rules, including prayers and Mass on Sunday with the family, became items for "discussions."

If there was a time when John and I felt least like the "missionaries" that Father talked about, it was during those years. Fortunately, we established our rules when our children were young, supported each other when needed on specific issues (you know the ones when the kids try to pit one parent against the other), and basically dug our heels in for the long haul. Our most effective weapons were prayer, attendance at daily Mass when possible, togetherness, and a *sense of humor*.

As my friend Vickey, mother of seventeen (she's no slouch!), once advised me, "Man the battle stations and full speed ahead, kid!"

I remember the year we were having nearly one hundred fifty relatives and friends for an open house in celebration of my parents' fiftieth wedding anniversary. We had prepared for weeks for the occasion. I made sure all our kids had clean and pressed suits and dresses for the anniversary Mass. I was thrilled at the thought that many out-of-town family members were coming and would be meeting my children for the first time.

So what did our son Tim do? (Why is it always him?) Two days before the gala event he took a bus across town to a hair "specialist" who shaved most of his head leaving little more than the *obvious* form of a "lightning bolt" on the sides, over each ear! So much for pride!

Actually, John and I are always secretly relieved when our children's rebellion or personal "statements" take the form of pierced ears, outrageous dress, or colored and unusual hair-dos. These acts are relatively harmless. In fact, it helps the kid vent frustration, show individuality, and sure beats drugs, alcohol, or promiscuous sexual behavior!

In Tim's case, the lightning bolt and shaved head quietly

disappeared once we registered the appropriate shock and he found other avenues to demonstrate his "uniqueness."

Four weeks before his high-school graduation, Tony walked through the door with an earring in his ear! Ten years ago I would have gone into my normal Italian tirades. But for what purpose? Here was my free-spirited Vietnamese son who was not a rebellious or bad boy but rather a good-natured fun-loving kid who would be graduating with honors and was headed for the university. After making our usual jokes about "Did anyone we know see you?" we figured that if he wanted another hole in his head, it was ultimately *he* and not we who would wear it. My reaction would have been far different, however, had Tony been twelve rather than eighteen at the time.

All in all, other than Vincent, who left home at sixteen, we've had few threats of mutiny during those difficult periods. In fact, we really enjoy having teens around the house. They are (in spite of their preoccupation with the bathroom mirror, the phone, and self) warm, witty, and quite forgiving.

And that's important to remember. We've made our share of mistakes along the way, and I for one have done my share of apologizing for my hot-tempered decisions and demands. I've never hesitated to say "I'm sorry" and ask forgiveness and when I've done so, my humility and willingness to go to the hurting child have only brought us closer together.

Can parents warp or permanently damage their kids, as some of the so-called child-care professionals would have us believe? Again, we've relied on our pastor's words that "parents cannot corrupt their children in areas of faith and morals, so long as they remain prayerful and faithful." Ain't that a relief?

2 ● THE PARENTAL ROLE IS ONE OF THE HIGHEST CALLINGS A HUMAN BEING CAN ASPIRE TO. The world seems to be caught up in a race toward destruction and death. Thinking of "me" has replaced all concepts of doing for others. It's no wonder, then, that the importance of the family and having children have come under attack and criticism. Ignore it all! Who wants to be in that kind of a race, anyway?

It may be hard to remember when we're knee-deep in diapers, dirty dishes, or discipline decisions, but we Christian mothers and fathers are doing something far more influential and powerful than any leader in the secular world. We have the power to shape the world for years — in fact, generations — to come, because it will be our children and our children's children who will become the future doctors and lawyers as well as business, political, and religious leaders. And a *frightening* world this would be if they didn't have faith!

Little surprise, then, that Catholics are so ridiculed and despised. Our faith upholds traditional marriage, welcomes children as a "blessing," and opposes abortion and artificial means of birth control as well as the rampant promiscuity others insist is a "lifestyle."

As Catholics we are called to put our faith in God, to obey his laws, and to be at least open to the possibility of new life, unless serious reasons prevail.

Some points we learned along the way:

✔ **Fathers take the lead.** Recent studies prove that in the area of faith, it is the father who will have the greatest impact on the children and the religious practices they will carry with them to adulthood.

In other words, the sons will imitate the father, and the daughters will generally choose a spouse *most like dad*.

This does not mean that a single mother, or a family in which the father is a nonbeliever, has an impossible task. It simply means the mother must "double her efforts."

In the case of the widowed or divorced, they should be encouraged to see Christ as their missing spouse and to turn to him for their strength and needs. We, too, have a special call, as the Bible says, to extend special care to "widows and orphans."

✔ **A united front is crucial.** Where spouses are of different religions, or one of the partners is unchurched, it is vital to give a witness of reverence and respect for the Catholic spouse's faith.

✔ **It's important that children see their parents in play, in prayer, and in love.** While it certainly is not harmful for children to witness an occasional disagreement or dispute and, in fact, it may be healthy in order that they get a full and more realistic view of marriage, still it is extremely important that they see their parents cuddle and openly demonstrate affection and love.

We Kuharskis believe in lots of "time-outs" for play — as a couple and with the family — sprinkled with lots of touching and hugs!

This hit home one day when our oldest daughter, Chrissy, was being interviewed by a reporter regarding her leadership of a campus pro-life group. "Are you involved in pro-life at St. Thomas because your parents are active in pro-life?" the reporter asked. "No. I'm doing it because it's my belief, too. But I don't mind being compared to my mom or dad," Chrissy responded. "I see them and the good friends they have, the fun they have together and the faith they share, and I know they are happy, fun people. Why wouldn't I want to be like them?"

✔ **God created men and women to complement one another.** By our very nature we are equal — yet different. We must never be afraid to accent these natural differences. It is up to us to let our children see in us strong roles they can emulate and use as models.

✔ **While the father is the head, the mother is the "heart" of the home.** An old-fashioned but true concept. The mother by her example, her very presence, transmits security, love, and a sense of well-being to her family. While a man's strengths may lie with rationality, logic, and professional processing, a woman is usually the more sensitive to the feelings, hurts, or vulnerabilities of others. Together, a husband and wife make quite a team. And that's the way God intended us to be!

I'm a firm believer in a "mother's intuition." In fact, I think intuition is a gift from God, bestowed the moment that first "little one" comes out of the womb.

Let's face it. Quite often it is a "well-tuned" mom who was perceptive enough to pick up on a teen's feelings of rejections, a young adult's job loss, or some kind of ensuing danger hovering around a curious and carefree child that was not allowed to fester or flourish because Mom "just knew."

Many a mom has saved a kid from death, disaster, or

dishonor just because "something told her" to get involved. That's Mom's intuition! (My kids say it's "spooky!")

✔ **Look to the Blessed Mother, a perfect role model.** The most important thing we contemporary parents, especially young mothers, can do is to ask Mary to teach us how to love Christ and to lead us to him. Mary wants to be our Mother, to listen to our cares, to take them to her Son, and to lead us to his waiting arms. It makes perfect sense to me. As a mother of seven boys, tot through teen, I know one thing: If someone wants a favor from one of my sons, it's a wise move to *ask me* to "put in a good word." So, too, I go to Mary.

3 ● ACTIONS SPEAK LOUDER THAN WORDS. LET OUR CHILDREN SEE OUR FAITH AND CHRISTIAN COMMITMENT. Children learn by observation and osmosis. A lesson clearly brought home to me when our daughter Mary Elizabeth (then eleven) wrote a paper on why she wanted to remain "smoke-free." "I want to remain smoke-free because you can get lung cancer, heart disease, emparzema [emphysema], and yellow fingers."

Although neither John nor I smoke (a habit I was once enslaved to), Mary had *observed* other smokers. What she noticed most and liked least was the yellow fingers! (Adults would probably be more concerned about lung cancer, heart disease, and "emparzema.")

Our children pick up far more by looking than by any lecturing, leading, or pleading we might do. If we lie in bed on Sunday and make up flimsy excuses for missing Mass; if we gamble, drink excessively, or overeat; if we brag about cheating on our taxes; if we gossip about our neighbors and friends, use profanity or display pornography; or worse yet, if we run down the pastor or Church teachings — if we do these things, our children will do the same.

So, too, in areas that affect not only the family but the community and society at large, our children must see our willingness to serve, to get involved, and to try to make a difference. This can be shown by our involvement with church work, charitable organizations, and even getting involved in the political process in order to work for lawmakers and laws that would uphold Judeo-Christian principles.

✔ **Babies are dying.** If there is any one issue of our time that demands our Christian witness and involvement, it is the issue of abortion. Our children must see by our votes, by our financial sacrifices to pro-life groups, and by our actions, that we are doing everything possible to restore legal protection to preborn babies and their mothers.

Speaking out *against* abortion shows our own children the high regard we have for them and all God's children. They are made in God's image and likeness, and God makes *no* mistakes.

We want our young to learn by our example that God has a plan and a purpose for them and that abortion thwarts his plan. I think the most stinging reminder of this came home to me after the adoption of our son Charlie, who had come from a Vietnamese orphanage.

I was trying to find a quiet corner in the house to prepare for a debate with a well-known Minnesota abortionist, scheduled to take place at a college campus the next morning. My opponent proudly boasted of running an "underground abortion business" before its legalization.

When Charlie and Tim (both aged seven then) came into the room to play, I quickly attempted to shuffle them off to another room. "Mom needs to be alone to study, boys," I pleaded.

"What are ya studyin', Mom?" Charlie asked.

I tried to brush him off with a quick response of "It's about abortion and I'll explain it to you later."

As they were leaving the room I heard Charlie ask his brother, "Tim, what's 'borshun?"

"Oh," Tim explained, "it's the way they get rid of the unwanted kids. They kill the babies before they get born."

A few minutes later, Charlie was back in the room. This time he just sat on the sofa opposite my chair and stared at me. Finally, when I could no longer ignore his piercing black eyes, I looked up and asked, "*Now* what do you want, Charlie?"

"I'm just glad I was born in *my* country and not America or they would have got me, too," he declared.

Referring to the abortionists, Charlie recognized that in spite of the fact that he came from an orphanage in a war-torn Communist country, which took the lives of his whole family, and in spite of the five and one-half years in which he witnessed bombings, shootings, burials in mass graves, and a hunger that ultimately demanded that he catch and consume animals we would consider household pets, this little guy felt he was better off than being born in America.

I realized then that not just for Charlie, and not just for the adopted children, but *for the sakes* of all of our children, we must speak out. Today's young are growing up as the first generation of Americans under a slogan that constantly reminds them that "unwanted children" can be legally killed.

If we *appear apathetic* or remain little more than "personally opposed," we've given them a message about the value we place on human life and ultimately their own lives. What kind of world do we want them to inherit? How we reverence and work to protect life is eventually how our children will do the same.

✔ **Attend Sunday Mass together as a family.** I know, I know. I'll be the first to admit that I've poured myself into the pew on many a Sunday morning when I've sung through gritted teeth and prayed over smoldering senses that were kicked out of shape by a last-minute mutiny or frenzied beginning. All the more important that we stand and kneel in common union before God's altar in prayer.

Personally, on the mornings I feel that only my body was present at church, while my mind and prayers were "in absentia," I've relied on the words of St. Augustine who says, "The mere intent to pray is a prayer."

God is so good. He'll take us any way he can get us. Just imagine. The mere fact that we *will* to pray is good enough for God!

✔ **Pray together before meals and at bedtime as a family.** It will be these moments — as hurried or harried as they may be — that will be remembered and eventually repeated by our young in the years to come.

Our older children, some of whom were once "doubting Thomases," are now the best role models for our little guys and girls coming up the ranks. Funny how faith mixed with a few years of maturity brings God into focus!

✔ **Make good use of pictures, statues, and sacramentals.** Just as photos displayed around a home remind us of loved ones, so also do statues and pictures. Little children love to see statues of the Holy Family and enjoy reading the lives of the saints. Most Catholic gift shops have an ample supply of such books that are written for the very young as well as adults. The saints are our spiritual heroes. How sad it is when our young know more about a football player or rock singer than they do about our illustrious saints. Get them a book as a special Christmas or Easter gift.

The first holy water font went up in our home after watching our son Michael dip his fingers into the little moon-shaped dish of water as we entered church each Sunday. But instead of reverently making the Sign of the Cross, he would quickly plunge the four dripping fingers into his mouth and suck off the water. He had no idea what the purpose of the holy water was.

Once we began using holy water to bless the children when they were going off for the first day of school, taking important exams, heading out for a long trip away from home, or when they were sick, we all felt a renewed and deeper appreciation of this special outward sign of our faith.

✔ **Create Catholic customs and celebrations to remember.** The Sacrifice of the Mass is the highest form of prayer. We want our children to know, too, that the sacraments are gifts from Christ to his Church and each time we receive or witness a sacrament, it is deserving of our reverence, respect, and rejoicing. The best way to let them know that, is to celebrate each baptism, First Holy Communion, confirmation, and wedding in a way that would be both fun and memorable. Our children all look forward to our baptism parties. Of course, there are those who suggest we had all these kids just because we love to party!

✔ **Catholic education is a must.** The most effective way to transmit the faith is not by talking about it but by living it. Children are great "copy cats." They're also very perceptive at picking up on shallowness and hypocrisy. Tell them you need God as the center of your life and then try to live it. Even when they see our imperfections, they'll know we're trying.

Secondly, we try to surround our family with loved ones

who mirror our faith and fundamental beliefs. Christian friends are a wonderful and positive reinforcement. They can also help us be on the lookout for any trouble spots.

Next, we made sure that our children received formal instruction in the Catholic faith. The best possible way to do that is to send them to Catholic schools. In some cases, that is not possible perhaps because of distance, finances, or the need for special-education courses that can only be obtained through public schools. In that event, most parishes offer evening or Sunday sessions known as Confraternity of Christian Doctrine, or CCD, classes.

Our children benefited immensely from both of these educational programs. They did more than learn about their religion; the classes brought them together with others who shared the same faith and fundamental beliefs. An added reinforcement for us as parents! And well worth the time and money invested.

✔ **Believe in your children: Let them feel your trust and love.** Kids will rise to greatness if they think we believe they can. Conversely, they will turn out like bums if we keep telling them we knew they would.

All children have their mischievous moments and make one or two momentous mistakes. Some more than others. A couple of ours seemed more prone to "collecting evil for a hobby," and yet we never let them think that we expected any less of them than the others. All of us, young and old, want to be forgiven, to have a second chance, and to save face from humiliation.

One of the ways I have found that helps young people climb back out of disruptive or destructive behavior is to make them take "time out" to think about what they're doing. Of course, I give them an extra job (like floor or wall washing) to speed the thinking process along!

I've often said to a misbehaving child (and this even includes a rebellious teen), "I don't recognize the kid I'm seeing right now. You've always been so helpful, so considerate, so thoughtful" (and any other "-fuls" I can think of that are positives).

"Did another kid climb in your skin when I wasn't looking? You better stick around the house here for a while until you can get rid of the kid that's causing all the trouble and bring back the son/daughter that I know and love. Right now I see only this awful person with an unhappy face who is doing all these naughty things. Take all the time you need to bring back the good kid that I know and love."

This technique has helped remind our children of our love and that we believe them more capable of good behavior. It also helps them climb out of what may become a destructive way of thinking and acting, that is, a bad behavior mold.

4 ● IN A SACRAMENTAL MARRIAGE GOD IS OUR THIRD PARTNER. The Catholic Church has always upheld the sacred union of husband and wife and reminds us constantly of the grace God offers to help us throughout our married lives.

God wants to be our Third Partner in all of our plans and decisions. Johnny and I continue to learn that it is only when we place ourselves in God's loving hands that our spiritual, physical, emotional, and financial needs will be met. And in a far better way than we ever dreamed possible. God is never outdone in generosity! The more we give to God, the more he lavishly showers blessings on us! Inviting God into our hearts and lives also means including God in our family-planning decisions.

It's funny how Christians claim to carry Jesus in their hearts, pray to and praise him on a daily basis, and look to God for help in every crisis, large or small; yet in the area of children — by far the greatest blessing and miracle in a married couple's life — they *tell* God how many children they will *accept*. I know all about that because for a time my husband and I did it, too.

The Catholic Church calls us to respect nature and, more importantly, God's law. Unless a husband and wife believe there are serious emotional, physical, familial, or financial conditions to consider, they are called to be *open* to the possibility of new life.

Pope John Paul II wrote in his Apostolic Exhortation on the Family: "Whenever Christian spouses in a spirit of sacrifice and trust . . . carry out their duties of procreation with generous human and Christian responsibility, they glorify the Creator and perfect themselves in Christ. . . . Special mention should be made of those who, after prudent reflection and common decision, courageously undertake the proper upbringing of a large number of children." Courageous is the key word here!

Personally speaking, our love and faith increased with each child. In fact, it was a three-day married couples' retreat and the simple question "Do you think you have all the children God intends you to have?" that initially made us realize that we had been limiting God and preventing him from working in our lives by declaring that "four is enough."

In our own case, there was no grave financial, emotional, or physical reason why we couldn't be open to the possibility of another. We began to pray and to trust in God's will for our lives. The rest is history.

I do recognize that not every married couple is called to parent a large family. For some, the fact that they *cannot* have children may be a far more difficult burden to bear.

Our "no more than two children" culture, however, suggests that most couples have limited themselves *and* God. All I'm suggesting is prayer and an openness to the will of God in family-planning decisions.

To answer the question "Do you think you have all the children God intends you to have?" Dr. Herb Rantner, a noted sociologist, author, and lecturer, says it best: "The greatest gift parents can give their child is not a new bike, a room of his own, or a college-paid education. No. The greatest gift they can give a child is the love of brothers and sisters." We agree!

3

❦

The Family That Works Together...

Father Patrick Peyton, the priest who traveled the globe encouraging Catholic devotion to the Rosary, coined the phrase "The family that prays together, stays together." This is one family that can vouch for the truth in that message.

And based on a few years' experience, and a "baker's dozen" of kids, I'd like to add: "The family that *works* together, stays together." Through our children, we've learned the value of expecting everyone to share in the household work and develop good work habits.

Our adopted son Charlie was five-and-one-half years old when he arrived from Cambodia. He was just recovering from scarlet fever and was still on medication, with one eye closed but seeping. His poor little mouth held rows of decaying teeth in need of immediate dental work; and to top it all off, he spoke not a word of English. We wanted him to feel welcome, and we treated him with caution and sensitivity.

Charlie was quick to notice our family routine and the harmony in both our work and our play. One Saturday, several weeks after he arrived, we were all busy at our usual chores when Charlie walked over and grabbed the vacuum out of his brother Tim's hands. Soon he and Tim were engaged in a tug-of-war over the machine.

He couldn't tell us in English words, but the message soon became clear: He *insisted* on vacuuming the stairs and hallway. Charlie no longer wanted to be a houseguest. He wanted to be *one of us.*

Charlie taught us all an essential lesson, one that I've often shared with other nervous adoptive parents: Pitching in to help makes children of any age feel they are a vital part of the family.

Sharing the load not only teaches youngsters responsibility and good work habits, but it makes them feel they are important.

When our friends Dave and Jean adopted a sibling group of three from South America, Jean became frantic when the oldest child, age nine, began to rebel against his new home and family.

"What can we do? He just can't seem to stay out of trouble," she confided.

"Does he have some assigned chores to do?" I asked.

"Well, not really," she responded.

"Do you have a dishwasher?" I asked.

"Yes, of course," she answered.

"I suggest you quit using it," I said. "Give the little guy the job of doing the supper dishes, even if he balks at first. With patience and praise he will see that you are expecting good things from him. Let him know that his bad behavior will not cancel his adoption or cause you to send him packing."

It worked! Jean called two weeks later to say her rebellious youth immediately "took charge" of his assigned tasks and that while his behavior was far from perfect, he had begun to demonstrate some consideration for his new parents and surroundings. "He's really trying to see where he fits in," she added.

Quite frankly, I think we parents do our youngsters a great disservice when we deny them the opportunity to be a working part of the family. Admittedly, my crew doesn't always view its chores as "golden opportunities." In fact, most of my bunch think they're the only ones in the world required to do so many jobs. Nevertheless, it is amazing the trust and responsibility that children demonstrate if given the opportunity.

Learned through our own trial and error, here are some more thoughts on kids and chores:

1 ● NEVER TAKE A CHORE OVER OR DO IT YOURSELF BECAUSE YOU CAN DO IT BETTER. Of course, you can do it better! But how else will a child learn? Love your children enough to let them learn.

The first house John and I bought needed electrical outlets installed throughout the basement. John's dad, who was retired, came over one day while John was at work and put in all the units. He was quite a handyman and really wanted to help. I thought it was great! I could now see what I was doing in the laundry and work area, and the kids had a well-lit section for play.

But when John came home from work, his face fell when I told him Dad had done all the wiring. "I don't know the first thing about wiring," John explained. "I wish he would have come on the weekend when I was home. Then I could have helped him do it and I would have learned how. Now I still don't know."

We're never too old to learn, and how much better to learn than working alongside an experienced parent or sibling.

2 ● GRANDMA'S OLD CLICHÉ STILL RINGS TRUE: "MANY HANDS MAKE LIGHT WORK." Children who share in the responsibility have a stake in the results. When everyone is working together, the chores seem less like work and can sometimes be downright fun.

3 ● ONE OF THE BEST WAYS TO FIND OUT WHAT A KID IS THINKING OR FEELING IS TO WORK ALONGSIDE HIM OR HER. Doing dishes together is a great conversation builder and can even break down hostility. I'll wash and assign drying to someone who is angry or "smoldering." With the number of dishes and pots and pans we do in an evening, even a monk on retreat would break down and talk after a while!

4 ● NEVER PAY A CHILD TO DO ROUTINE CHORES. Dr. John Rosemond, noted psychologist and author, contends that when parents pay children for performing chores, they create the illusion that if the children don't want the money, they don't have to do the work. Also, when children are being paid for helping, the chores are no longer a means of contribution but a means of blackmail.

Although some large jobs (like painting the house, roofing, and other time-consuming or heavy tasks) may appropriately deserve pay, we don't believe children should receive an allowance for sharing in the normal responsibility of maintaining a clean and orderly home. After all, we're talking family here — not "minimum wage." No child (except a toddler, perhaps) should be exempt from participating in routine family chores.

When it comes to money, our rule is that we should "be careful how freely we hand it out to our young." We believe that children, no matter their ages — including teens, college students, or young adults living at home — should never be handed an "allowance" or vast sums of money, whether it's to assist in their education or to see them through a crisis. We can stifle their potential and self-determination when we don't allow them the privilege (and responsibility!) of earning their way, working it off, or paying back a loan.

5 ● "CHORES ARE THE GLUE THAT BONDS CHILDREN TO THE VALUES AND TRADITIONS OF THE FAMILY." So says Dr. Rosemond. This is one family in the "trenches" that couldn't agree more!

We've witnessed a definite sense of cohesiveness as our own "melting pot" family has learned to pray, play, and work together.

Along with the sheer rhythm and routine of performing the same tasks on a daily and weekly basis, there comes an overall sense of purpose that reminds each that he or she is vital to this unit. The children come to believe that their presence really does make a difference.

Dr. Rosemond asks, "Where in this country have family values and traditions been passed along most reliably from generation to generation?" The answer: in rural America. And what distinguishes the lives of children raised on farms from the lives of children raised in urban settings? The answer: chores. I like the way this guy thinks!

6 ● MY MOTHER USED TO SAY: "IT TAKES LONGER TO DO IT WRONG THAN IT DOES TO DO IT RIGHT." Most if not all children will try to rush through or get by with a slipshod job. Don't let them. This is the training ground for their future habits and attitude in the workforce.

There are times when John and I have to make a kid do a job over, and over, and over, because the task was done in a careless and sloppy manner.

One son was notorious for "failing inspection" and having

to repeat floor-washing, bathroom-cleaning, and lawn-clipping assignments. Many a time we were as frustrated and impatient with him as he was with us when he had to redo a job. I got so tired of always having to recheck his work and then bringing him back into the bathroom, bedroom, or kitchen to point out the areas he "missed." Yet we realized that if we let him get by with it as a child, his slipshod attitude would remain with him the rest of his life. No employer would be willing to pay a full day's wages for a half day's work!

7 ● CHILDREN OVER TWELVE SHOULD HAVE SOME SOURCE OF OUTSIDE INCOME. There are plenty of jobs for kids who want to work and earn money — even for those living in the big city. Our children take a once-a-week paper route, do outside baby-sitting, or solicit yard work or housecleaning jobs from neighbors. This helps them become responsible, dependable, and reliable. It's also a good beginning to learn money management.

8 ●PUT A MISCHIEVOUS YOUNGSTER OR REBELLIOUS TEEN TO WORK AND KEEP HIM OR HER BUSY! We've had more than our fair share of naughty, mischievous, or rebellious kids. Several seemed to have no turn-off valve for their energy. It didn't take long to realize that merely grounding them or giving them time-outs for misbehavior only helped to store that energy for another episode. Instead, we began to put that energy to work.

At times when one of our kids — be it a rebellious teen, impish adolescent, or hyper five-year-old — got into trouble, I gave that individual a job. I made sure it wasn't an easy or fun job but one he or she would remember and one the youngster wouldn't be anxious to repeat. Washing walls; scrubbing the deck with soap and water; scouring the stains from the pots and pans; waxing floors; washing and polishing woodwork; pulling weeds and spading the garden — these are just a few of my "creative correction chores."

Giving the kids a task as punishment for bad behavior also gives them the opportunity to do something good and to receive praise for a job well done. I use the occasion then to remind the involved children that this is how we see them, as individuals who do good things and not inconsiderate or bad things. A job well done — even if accomplished as retribution — offers kids a chance for praise, and allows them to climb out of that bad-behavior rut.

9 ● TEACH CHILDREN TO WORK PRAYERFULLY. St. Paul tells us to "pray always." Our Catholic faith teaches that every single act of the day can become a prayer for the honor and glory of God, if we intend it to be. Thus no act, no chore, no task, is insignificant or meaningless in God's eyes if we give it to him in prayer. My kids — "saints in the making" though they may be — still moan and groan when I announce it's time for "spring cleaning" or other big projects. Yet they all know my response to their whining: "Offer it up."

10 ● A CLEAN AND ORDERLY HOME GIVES HONOR AND GLORY TO GOD. It's more than good training and obedience. Our actions show reverence and gratitude for the many blessings and goods God has generously placed in our care.

4

❦

Discipline Is Love

Sometimes I feel like my vocation is nothing more exciting than replacing toilet-paper rolls, unraveling soiled socks that are aimlessly tossed down the clothes chute, or chipping out the ground-in gum and other questionable "remains" from the family-room carpet — all left by a bunch of ungrateful little bodies! Before I get too absorbed in self-pity, however, I have to admit that if I'm feeling a bit walked on it's because I was lying down on the job and allowing it to happen.

For those of us involved in family life, it's important to keep in mind what the Church teaches about the role of parenting: (1) Parents have an obligation to nurture, love, educate, and encourage their children in faith. (2) For their part, children have an obligation to be obedient and to show honor and respect to their parents. This does not, by the way, end at age eighteen!

After twenty-plus years of mothering, I'm convinced that discipline is truly a form of love. I am also convinced that many parents today are *afraid* to discipline their children. As a result, kids will go to all kinds of extremes — including the most wretchedly bad behavior — as a means of forcing a parent to show he or she cares enough to discipline.

Psychologist and author John Rosemond says, "Children show respect for their parents by obeying them. Parents show respect for their children by insisting that they obey." I'm with him. The trick is putting it into practice.

Most parents admit to days when they'd just as soon "look the other way" or say "yes" when it should be "no" because in the short run it's just plain easier. In the long run, however, it's the overindulged child, testy teen, or unmanageable youngster (that few find pleasant to be around) who causes all kinds of grief.

My husband and I have gone from amateur-and-pushover to polished-and-professional, thanks to the thirteen kids who raised us. We entered parenthood just barely out of "kid-hood" ourselves, yet managed to survive and thrive from our varied crew of siblings basically by keeping the following principles in mind:

✔ **Children want to be good.** They want to see themselves as *being good*. And they want others — especially parents, grandparents, and other loved ones, as well as those in authority — to see them the same way. In fact, I've never met a kid who wants to be known as a terrorist or a brat. Some, however, are. It doesn't happen overnight; rather, it is built up gradually as the child comes to the realization that negative behavior brings the attention so craved.

When I'm disciplining a youngster for bad behavior, I'll give him or her a job such as scrubbing a wall, washing the floor, or chopping ice off the walks. Thus the child has a chance to get out of the "doghouse" by doing something good, and I can praise him or her for a job well done, helping us all end the ordeal on a positive note.

✔ **If we really let our children know we expect them to obey — they will.** The follow-through is to love them enough to discipline when they don't obey. It sounds simple, and yet most of us know parents who repeatedly argue with their children. They make empty and outrageous threats of punishment that they and their children know they have no intention of carrying out.

✔ **We say what we mean and mean what we say.** Never promise, be it a reward or punishment, unless we intend to follow through. Thus the child learns early to accept your word as the truth and something worthy of respect.

✔ **Husbands and wives — be consistent and united.** If you disagree with your spouse on an issue of discipline, curfew, or privileges, don't let your child *capitalize* on the tension by playing one against the other. Children need and deserve clear, concise, and consistent messages.

✔ **Democratic rule in family life leads to chaos and confusion.** One-member-one-vote is a setup for disaster and creates the notion that the child has as much authority as the parents. Children are happiest when they are *allowed* to be children. Even when they *appear* to grab for the reins, they are relieved to know the responsibility is not theirs.

✔ **All children, including teens, need and want guidelines and rules.** In fact, limits and restrictions offer youngsters an assurance of safety and security. After all, they *are only kids*, and have had too little experience to weigh all factors or to begin to understand what some of the consequences of wrong decisions may be. How many parents have asked a mischievous or naughty child, "Didn't you think about what would happen?" And the answer is usually always a truthful "No."

Unlike adults, adolescence is marked by signs of short-range planning and split-second decisions. Just ask any kid left with too many "choices" about split-second decisions — be it water-skiing in winterlike weather, trying that first cigarette, skipping school, taking that first drink, or doing "it" once and getting pregnant! "I didn't think. . ." is the answer you'll hear most often.

Long-range planning and soulful analysis are reserved for those who make it to maturity and adulthood. If it were any different, we big people could be the kids and the little people could boss us around!

A Minneapolis family psychologist tells the story of one young girl who was becoming increasingly promiscuous in her behavior. She wrote details of her dating antics in her diary and, one day, left the diary on the bathroom counter in plain sight where her mother was sure to pick it up and read it. When the mother got to the last page, she read: "Why won't you tell me to stop this?" Why indeed!

✔ **Firmness tempered with a heavy dose of love and touch is crucial to a child's well-being.** A "time-out" or scolding (in some cases, a quick spanking) for a preschooler; for older children a grounding, taking the car keys away, or "whatever works" — such forms of discipline may be the most loving thing we can do. It's a crucial reminder that parental rules and regulations are not meant to hurt but rather to protect children from harm (be it physical, emotional, or spiritual).

Preschoolers *usually* comprehend a "time-out" or scolding, but on occasion a swift swat on the bottom is more effective than other forms of discipline. I would never use an object, however. The hand is stern enough.

I know the controversy over whether or not to spank; but, as I say, I'm for touch — both firm and loving. Our newly adopted five-and-a-half-year-old black/Cambodian son, Charlie, who could understand no English when he first arrived, taught me the value of spanking. He had been with us for three weeks and, like any normal youngster, had begun to "test" our hospitality. We initially responded with stern looks or finger-shaking "No, no's," but one morning he was playing with the hose and sprinkler and turned it on our unsuspecting neighbor as she hung her wash on the clothesline. I ran outside yelling and shaking my finger and finally, in frustration, gave him a swift swat on his backside. I turned around as I walked back into the house to catch the slight smile come across his tear-streaked face. If looks could speak, his face was saying to his brother Tim, who stood close by, "I must be here to stay 'cuz she's treating me like 'family.' "

My husband, John, and I have found that enforcing "time-out" penalties or grounding (and assigning some extra tasks to help them work off the excess energy) works best with school-age or older youngsters.

I happen to be one of those "mean" parents who demand and expect much from the young in their charge. I believe in firmness tempered with a heavy dose of love and *touch* — an-all-but-forgotten commodity in a culture that emphasizes "privacy" and "space." Perhaps it's my Italian nature, but I truly believe we should be holding, hugging, and squeezing our young — and this includes our teenagers — on a daily basis.

It might not be easy (or enticing) to grab that adolescent and offer a hug; but, believe me, they want and need affection — now more than ever.

Can you remember when you were that age? It was a time when most of us spent three quarters of our waking moments worrying about how best to measure up to our peers (not parents). The mere eruption of a new crop of pimples only increased our pain and self-consciousness. And, oh, the humiliation if we weren't asked to the latest party or dance. If anyone needs to feel loved and accepted, it's a teenager — give yours a squeeze often!

✔ **"Our home is our castle."** If they live under our roof, they must abide by our rules and respect our

judgment. It may not look like a castle to others, but to us it is! Thus we've told our kids that "every poster on the wall, every television show, every room in the house reflects *our* values as well as theirs. We can't allow something that is offensive or strikes at our faith and beliefs. Not in our castle."

✔ **Honor your mom and dad.** Even good parents can become intimidated and rendered ineffective by the presence of "bigger-than-us" children. We've found that all children — from adolescents to young adults — need parental guidance and discipline. It doesn't stop at a magic age.

My kids are no different. At the age of "maturity" (I use the term loosely), they've all tried the "I'm old enough to decide for myself" routine. And sometimes they are. But not in our house if it contradicts our faith and morals — it's not allowed. Thus I've removed "unfriendly" wall posters, taken away (what I consider to be) offensive music, and turned off naughty television programs — no matter how "award-winning" the show. Some of my children's line of argument can get downright creative. One even said he was watching a TV "skin flick" as a school assignment!

I'm so tyrannical I even forbid daytime TV, Nintendo (too habit-forming and time-consuming — dulls their active brains), or personal TV sets. One of my more clever kids tried hiding a small set in his room. I fined him twenty-five dollars and sent the set packing! Needless to say, booze, drugs, or anything that would remotely suggest illegal or immoral behavior is not tolerated. Neither is sassing back or bad language.

An acquaintance of mine, a mother of three active teens, confided in frustration to a few of us over coffee one day about the television-viewing habits of her young: "I don't know what to do. They watch such violent shows — and some that are pretty sexually explicit. I feel like I can't say anything because I'm dealing with older kids now. I mean they're fourteen-, sixteen-, and nineteen-year-olds. Last night I got up and said I was walking out because the program so disgusted me. I went in the other room and sat on an uncomfortable chair while they all stayed watching on easy chairs in the family room. What do I do?"

Ginny, another friend and a grandmother with experience, bluntly responded, "Turn off the tube. That's what I'd do! It's your home and your television and the things that are watched, read, and listened to, represent *you* more than your kids. Tell them that *that* kind of material does *not* reflect your faith or values and that you have a right to turn it off when it's in your home because you find it offensive." Ginny is right.

✔ **Keep the lines of communication open.** I'm most grateful for "been there" friends whose shared experiences became a source of support and strength when we began to encounter a new phase of "firsts" in our parenting years — namely the teenage and young adult years.

Our friends Pat and Jack showed us what *real* love meant when they watched one of their young adults "jump" the nest early and then a year later lovingly offered their forgiveness and the option to return home for a second chance. "Always keep the lines of communication flowing — even when you don't feel like it," she confided. Still, what parent is ever really prepared when it happens to him or her?

One of our sons (then nineteen) decided to leave home to live at a fraternity near the University of Minnesota. He wanted *freedom* rather than conforming to our curfews and rules. I cried for a week (Italians are such clingers!). It was my friend Dorothy who wisely advised, "Call him up. Invite him for dinner."

Dorothy was right. The lines were definitely *strained* and there was a real "leave me alone" distancing for the next two years, yet I believe our parent/son relationship is good today because we did not let our pride or rigidity get in the way. He knew he was always welcome and many a Sunday dinner kept him coming back.

✔ **The power of prayer and a reliance on God's grace can pull us through any situation.** Time and faith do heal — even in what appears to be the most insurmountable instances.

All kids make mistakes. When it's a serious yet first-time offense, we let ours know that "God forgives and so do we."

A good example is the time one of our boys (who will remain nameless to protect his penitent heart) came home drunk. Very drunk. We were awakened to discover not only a "sick" kid but also later learned that he had totaled his car as a result of hitting a tree! (Thank God he survived the wreck with hardly a scratch.) That evening brought a flood of emotion. No parent wants a kid fresh out of high school to be booted out. Most of us want to help offer a little "start in life," especially if college or trade school is being pursued.

Parents know only too well what kind of world awaits young people, and we'd like to spare them some of the disappointments, difficulties, and disorder. Forgiveness, some form of retribution (such as curfews and taking away driving privileges — even if it's the kid's own car), and the offer of a second chance give a young adult the means to climb back out and try again. If such behavior becomes a pattern, however, he or she must leave or voluntarily enter some program designed to help troubled individuals.

We are Catholics and, as such, we believe our parental obligation in areas of faith and morals continues as long as our children are living at home. We may have no control over behavior outside the home, but we are "in control" and will be accountable for what we allow to occur while they live under our roof.

Speaking personally regarding young adults living at home, Johnny and I offer little financial backing for our college-age young. We offer free room and board (as long as they are in school and holding part-time employment).

This is their time now to begin their own preparation for the exodus that will come when they strike out on their own. What better beginning than to feel the self-reliance that comes with *working* their way through college! In return for free lodging (those not in school are expected to work full-time and pay room and board), all our children, including young adults, must attend Mass on Sunday and holy days; they must join us at mealtime and prayertime if they are home; they must keep reasonable curfews (no all-night busts, unlawful drinking, driving, drugs, or promiscuity); and *everyone* must pitch in with household chores.

✔ **"The secret to raising happy, healthy children is to pay more attention to your marriage than you do to the kids."** This is what Dr. John Rosemond insists. He also says that today's parents are so overly involved in the recreation of their children that their recreation is no longer play but "performance." If you've ever attended a Little League game, watched a Junior Miss Pageant, or sat through a dance recital, you'd agree.

"It is important," he says, "that the worlds of adults and children be distinct and often exclusive."

My husband, John, makes sure we get out together *alone* once a week, be it to a nice restaurant for dinner or just a walk to the ice-cream shop for a late-night snack. In addition, we've been faithful to a commitment we made since BK (before kids) to get away on a vacation *alone* every year.

Occasionally, the kids object. John kiddingly tells our young, "This isn't our vacation. It's yours! We're doing this for you guys!" And, in a way, it's true. We firmly believe that God uses those little times away to rejuvenate, refresh, and renew our married love.

Whether it's a scant twenty-four hours at a nearby resort, or a week under the Mexican moon, there is something mysterious and marvelous that happens to a husband and wife who leave home, work, and surroundings to be with each other. It's more than a honeymoon — it's a renewed commitment to each other and to that vital *mission* of parenting.

Occasionally, we've come home to find kids who have surprisingly learned the hard way that our discipline and rules "aren't so bad after all." Like the time one baby-sitter decided she'd had enough from one of our teens who had an "attitude problem." She assigned him the task of chopping ice around all the drain spouts in sub-zero weather. "A woman after my own 'stony' heart" — I always say!

Think back to your favorite teacher or adult mentor. Usually your mind flips, not to the pushover, the "Mr. Nice Guy," but rather to the one who demanded much, disciplined fairly, and generously praised when a job was done well. As parents acting with love we can do no less!

5

❦

Spiritual Survival for Mom and Dad

One of the greatest challenges to family life — whether you're parenting one or many — is getting the housework and family chores done without feeling overwhelmed by it all. This may be especially true for those bringing home a new baby, recovering from sickness or surgery, working outside the home, or parenting without a spouse.

While I wouldn't begin to offer a surefire solution or schedule for squeezing it all in with ease, the following advice has been the greatest help to me — especially during periods when the demands of everyday life seem to press from every side.

1 ● BEGIN EACH DAY WITH A PRAYER. Offer each and every act — little or big, joyful or dreadful — as a prayer offering to God.

St. Paul in his epistles repeatedly encourages the faithful to "pray always" and "pray unceasingly." In order to do that we must learn to commit *every* act as a gift of prayer to God.

St. John Vianney — better known as the Curé of Ars, and most noted as the priest who would spend up to sixteen hours a day in the confessional listening, healing, and helping those who came to him — said, "Prayer is nothing less than union with God."

2 ● ATTEND DAILY MASS WHENEVER POSSIBLE. Without a doubt, the greatest gift to our marriage and personal lives came when Johnny and I began to attend daily Mass. The Sacrifice of the Mass is nothing less than a hidden source of grace and strength. In today's demanding age, what married couple doesn't need grace and strength on an everyday basis?

The decision to go to daily Mass was not a deliberate

decision, mutually made, but rather a routine we both seemed to "fall into" (if you believe in accidents or coincidences). Months after I had been going to daily Mass at our local parish, I learned that Johnny was attending Mass on his lunch hour downtown. Actually, I think our guardian angels had been quietly nudging us simultaneously. They knew we'd bitten off more than a chunk in what seemed like an impossible attempt to raise all these kids!

We now agree it was the Sacrifice of the Mass, which the Church calls the greatest prayer of all, that kept us spiritually, emotionally, and even physically healthy. We feel far more secure in meeting whatever challenges (and challenges we've had) come our way.

3 ● ON THE DAYS IT ALL SEEMS OVERWHELMING, MAKE A CHORE LIST AND BREAK IT INTO THREE SECTIONS: (1) Those things that *must* be done today, that is, doctor's appointments, diapers, dishes, laundry, housecleaning, or making meals (with thirteen kids, there's no such thing as "We'll just order out tonight!"). (2) The things that *should* get done but can possibly be put off for another day, that is, hanging new curtains, attacking a pile of mending, ironing (always a great postponer), cleaning the basement or toy room, or phoning for the church bake sale. (3) The *I'd-like-to-get-it-done* list. These are the chores that linger in the back of our mind and make us feel we have "a million things to do" — yet, when carefully thought out, they're not vital. In other words, shopping for next month's birthdays; wallpapering, putting up new curtains (why does that seem such a job?); or organizing that neighborhood recycling drive you talked about — these really *can* be postponed for a while. On the other hand, preparing a nice dinner and cleaning the house cannot. Especially if company is coming.

My cardinal rule is that if the house is clean, family members as well as guests are very understanding about walls waiting for paint, windows without curtains, or rooms in the midst of renovating.

Most moms of many, like myself, are frequently asked, "How in the world do you keep your house clean?" My response is, "It may not be spotless, but I do try to keep it picked up and in some kind of order — for my own peace of mind."

Once dishes are done, beds are made, and I know things are in relative order, my head is free to do some serious brainwork, like figure out when Dorothy and I can go to lunch, or write an editorial for *Prolife Minnesota*, the newsletter of the educational group I do volunteer work with.

All in all, my household philosophy and tips include:

✔ **Our home is our "castle."** Be it ever so humble, I do strive to make our surroundings pleasing, comfortable, clean, and attractive. Not only because it sets a good example for our children, but keeping a clean home is good stewardship. We, by our actions, demonstrate our gratitude to God for the gifts that have been so generously bestowed upon us.

✔ **There is an old saying: "Cleanliness is next to godliness."** When homemaking tasks become too tedious and tiresome to tackle, don't try to clean everything at once, but take it room by room, beginning with the ones closest to the front and back doors. There are days I may not get the entire house done, but those areas seen first by others will look fresh and friendly.

✔ **A clean and orderly environment allows me to feel there is an order, purpose, and accomplishment.** It may not be perfect, but keeping things picked up makes me feel I'm in control. (And name me an Italian mother who doesn't like to be "in control"!)

✔ **My day begins with a Morning Offering.** And hopefully my children will do the same. This prayer — giving our day and all we think, do, and say to God — is a beautiful way to open the day. We place ourselves and our intentions in God's control — and no one else's. One version of the Morning Offering goes like this: "O Jesus, through the Immaculate Heart of Mary, I offer you all my prayers, works, joys, and sufferings of this day for all the intentions of your most Sacred Heart in union with the holy Sacrifice of the Mass throughout the world, in reparation for my sins, for the intentions of all our associates, and in particular, for the intentions of the Holy Father."

In addition to daily Mass, my favorite everyday prayers (besides the Morning Offering) are:

"Dear Jesus, please come into my heart and take over my life today."

* * *

"Help me, Jesus, to do, as Mother Teresa says, something beautiful for God today."

* * *

"All for thee, O Sacred Heart of Jesus." (A phrase that can be said throughout the day, making every undertaking a prayer.)

6

❦

Sunday: Restoring the Day of Rest

It's often been enviously said that the generations before us had it easier because of the simplicity and serenity they enjoyed in comparison to the high-tech, fast-paced, "me-oriented" culture of today. Yes, life was simpler and perhaps less worrisome to the parents of yesteryear, who had little fear their children would be swept into cults, gangs, drugs, illicit sexual experiences, or caught up in the kind of selfishness that leaves little room for God and family.

Yet today's families have the luxury of leisure — a commodity that was rare or virtually unknown to our American ancestors who struggled sometimes for their very survival. On the other hand, unless it is plotted, planned, and premeditated, today's families enjoy little free time in common.

In our own case, we began to notice that as our youngsters moved into their preteen, teen, and young adult years, their free hours became filled with sports, paper routes, baby-sitting, part-time jobs, and *friends*.

Before we knew it, our dinner table always had several "missing in action." Eating on the run became the norm for these go-getters, and that once-taken-for-granted family dinner hour became occasional or nonexistent. It didn't take long before we realized that a disconnectedness and distancing was replacing the unifying time that we had daily assumed would always be.

I must say, none of the projects that took our kids' time and attention — be it athletics, social, musical, or academic — were bad. They were just time-consuming.

After all, there's nothing wrong with dancing, gymnastics, piano, saxophone, drums (ugh!), football, baseball, Little League, volleyball, basketball, soccer, track, band, Junior Achievement, tennis, wrestling, Scouts, Indian Guides (I think I'm running my own troop!), or "hanging out with friends" (questionable at least!) after school. It's just that the kids can't do it *all* and they can't do it *every* day!

"The problem we have here," I said to John one day, "is that these kids — the little ones as well as the bigger ones — could be involved with programs and schedules twenty-four hours a day if we don't put some kind of curb on this *now*." And so we did.

After we began to put a limit on their "extracurriculars," we at least knew who was coming home and when for supper. And, if not, why not. So we told them, "There are so precious few leisure hours when we can all be together. Family should come first. Let's be sure what we're doing is not causing more division than unity."

In order to restore some sense of togetherness and playtime, John and I became determined that at least *one* day a week would be reserved for family. And what better day than Sunday — the day set aside by the Church to be one of rest and recreation? Committed to making Sundays special we resolved the following:

✔ **No big chores or work projects would be done on Sunday.** Our heavenly Father created the whole universe in six days and rested on the seventh. He commands us to do the same.

✔ **Make Sunday special by the clothes we wear to church, to the dinner table, and throughout the day.** This is the Lord's day. Our dress as well as our attitude demonstrates to our children and to others that Sunday is special.

Children — both young boys and girls — love to dress up in something special. It doesn't have to be new — just special. Let them look to Sunday as the day they get to wear the dress shirt and hand-me-down bow tie, or the matching bonnet and purse.

My friend Dorothy set the stage early with her three children and held to her "Sunday-best" clothes rule in spite of those who predicted her young would wear her down.

"So many warned me, 'Just wait till they're teenagers and want to wear jeans,' " Dorothy related. " 'You'll never get them to dress up for Mass.' Oh, yeah?" She proved her critics wrong.

While the teen years may have presented their own set of challenges, "dressing up on Sunday was not up for debate or discussion. In fact, my kids, even then, liked looking special for church," Dorothy said.

Sometimes parents set themselves up for failure by *assuming* kids' rebellion in advance. Dorothy and Mike acted as if their children's cooperation was a given. And it was.

✔ **Attend Mass together as a family.** I can't stress the importance of this enough — even if it means walking out to the vestibule with a cranky baby, or incurring the hassles of an independent-minded teen. In the long run, our children *need* to see us worship God and to feel a part of our prayer commitment — even if we can't see the immediate benefits.

St. John Vianney once said, "Private prayer is like straw scattered here and there: if you set it on fire, it makes a lot of little flames. But gather these straws into a bundle and light them, and you get a mighty fire, rising like a column into the sky; public prayer is like that." (Maybe he was the originator of the phrase "Light my fire!")

✔ **Unless part-time jobs for teens or special occasions arise, everyone should try to be present for Sunday dinner.**

✔ **Make mealtime special.** Be it dinner at home, a backyard cookout, or a shared meal at an inexpensive restaurant, let your children grow up remembering Sunday as a day set aside for family and fun.

✔ **Turn off the tube and plan something fun.** Bring out the cards or game boards. Monopoly, Trivial Pursuit, Scrabble, Yahtzee, Canasta, home movies, or looking through family photo albums or kids' scrapbooks are a few indoor activities our family enjoys doing. Swimming, water-skiing, picnics, bowling, ice-skating, bike-riding, and walking are some outdoor activities.

✔ **How about a religious for dinner?** Sunday is a great time to invite a favorite priest or religious for dinner. Catholics often talk about praying for an increase in vocations. What better way for our children to know more about a religious than to get to know a priest, sister, or brother? Seeing those with a religious calling in a casual and relaxed setting is even more valuable.

✔ **Take time to visit family members or close friends.** Sunday for us has always been the day to stop by to visit the grandparents. It was a routine we began even before we had children and, as our family grew in size and in age, it became even more important to keep those ties strong.

We've been more fortunate than most, having had both of our parents living within a two-mile walking distance from our house. Even though we saw our parents on a weekly basis over the years, we were not quite ready when they died and were taken from our midst.

"It sure seems odd not to stop by Grandma K's," more than one of our youngsters remarked even months after her death. We were so very grateful that our lives and our leisure never got so full that we would look back in sorrow at what we didn't do to show our love and respect.

If you are fortunate enough to live near a grandparent or extended family member — especially if he or she is up in years — take the kids over for a visit. Most likely, it'll make the rest of that loved one's week!

✔ **Tithing.** Roman Catholics are just beginning to learn the value of tithing, that is, giving ten percent of their earnings to God. It is suggested that five percent go to charity and five percent to the parish. Most Catholic families who tithe, as difficult as that may be on a stretched budget and limited income, begin to experience untold blessings. Johnny and I quickly learned, through tithing, the old adage, "God can never be outdone in generosity." Moreover, encourage the children who have an income to share a portion with the church.

✔ **Forget what fast-paced times we live in.** Claim Sunday as "Family Day" at your house. You won't be sorry. I'm convinced that most of the world's "me-oriented" loners-by-choice would envy the enthusiasm, energy, and enjoyment pouring out of a family that does as God commands: "Keep holy the Sabbath day."

We Christians, by our lives and our leisure, should let the rest of the world know that we enjoy life and know how and when to take time out for worship and for fun!

7

❦

Dinnertime Blessings

There is something about dinnertime with the family that brings a blessing all its own. Meal-sharing is vital to a healthy family life. Especially in this fast-paced, eat-on-the-run, "me-oriented" culture. Praying before eating has become second nature at our house. In fact, we're so used to doing it, we make no apologies (excluding a mortified teen or two) for saying prayers when dining out or at others' homes.

When we consider the many ways that Christ used food and meals to demonstrate his love, we parents should do everything we can to make eating together not just happen but also an occasion of love.

It was no coincidence that Christ began his public ministry and performed his first miracle at a banquet — the marriage feast at Cana.

It was also at dinner that Christ called Matthew, a despised tax collector and sinner, to be one of his apostles. There's room at God's table for every repentant sinner! And so, too, it was at a meal, while he dined as a houseguest, that the penitent woman first encountered Christ, washed his feet, and received his forgiveness and love.

Later, in the miracle of the loaves and fishes, Christ again shows the importance of eating in community (or common unity, as I like to call it). While the Twelve Apostles pleaded with him to disperse the hungry crowd of five thousand, our Lord, ignoring their advice, instructed his followers to "make them sit down in groups of about fifty each." After all were settled, Jesus took "the five loaves and the two fish, . . . looked up to heaven, and blessed and broke them, and gave them to the disciples to set before the crowd" (see Luke 9:12-17). Twelve baskets of "leftovers" were gathered up after all had eaten. The meal — though large by any standards — became a unifying and a blessed event.

And, of course, the Last Supper, the very first Sacrifice of the Mass, was chosen by Christ as the one and *only* means to be used by his Church to pass on his *real* presence through the consecrated bread and wine.

Throughout Scripture Christ used food and meal-sharing to demonstrate his love. What a wonderful and built-in opportunity for parents! Christ calls us to make these occasions a time of relaxation, faith-sharing, and togetherness. Occasionally, you may notice, as we have, your own little miracle of healing, forgiveness, understanding, and love.

Speaking from more personal experience than I care to reveal, however, mealtime with small children can be anything but tranquil. If it's not a fussy baby or spilled milk (a *given* at every Kuharski meal), it's adolescents juggling piano schedules, paper routes, sports activities, and so on.

Yet we parents must remember that this hour in our day is a gift from God to be used as a special time of togetherness and love. It may not be perfect, but we can strive to give it the focus and priority it deserves. Some rules that have helped us:

✔ **Keep dinnertime a time for food and fun, laughter and love.** This is no place to solve financial binds, mollify "tantrummed" tots, or resolve teen troubles. No long lectures or nagging inquiries allowed.

✔ **No television or radios.** This may be the only time of the day — or week — when family members have the opportunity to hear about the happenings of others. World events can wait!

✔ **No eating separately unless jobs, school, extracurricular activities, or previous plans require it.** Those who are home — teens and young adults included — should be present at the evening meal.

✔ **Every meal begins with prayer.** Even the food will taste better, and the conversation is guaranteed more peaceful — spilled glasses and all!

In addition to the "Bless Us, O Lord" prayer we encourage our kids to read or recite another of their choice. In fact, we keep handy a typed-up prayer sheet with some of our favorite *"short"* prayers. It's been covered with plastic (need I say why?) and has become almost a permanent fixture at evening meals, with the little ones taking turns and being the most eager to do the evening "add-on."

Be careful of those new readers! We had one eager second grader who announced before dinner one evening her plans to do a "new" prayer. The whole family patiently sat, watching mashed potatoes, gravy, and once-warm roast beef turn cold and crusty, while she trudged through — word by stuttery word — the entire Apostles' Creed. From then on, new prayer selections had to be approved — in advance!

Remember, coming together at the evening meal may be the first haven of refuge and relief for parents and children since leaving home in the morning for school, jobs, pressures, and peers. With little effort, we can make this opportunity a time of leisure, laughter, and love.

8

Mary, Our Mother

A young woman I knew, a business acquaintance, called one day. She said she had just finished reading a book about the Blessed Virgin Mary and Medjugorje and wanted to talk.

"I never before understood devotion to Mary," she said. "I have no problem accepting Mary as the Mother of Christ and my heavenly Mother. But for the first time I realized that I can turn to Mary in prayer and she'll help me."

"And who better to plead our case," I told her, "than the Mother of God? Devotion to the Blessed Mother will only bring us closer to Christ," I told her. My friend agreed.

None of this would be unusual except for the fact that this young woman is not Catholic. "We Catholics don't have a corner on the Blessed Mother. We just like to *think* we do," I told her.

Devotion to Mary is not a new phenomenon but is really as old as the Church itself. It began with Christ at the crucifixion, when he looked down from the cross to his Mother and said, "Woman, here is your son." Then, looking at John, his beloved apostle, he told him, "Here is your mother" (see John 19:26-27). From that moment on, Mary became the Mother to all humankind.

When I was young and attending Catholic school, the sisters who taught us urged us to become "most Mary-like" in our thoughts, words, and actions.

In our young minds, we knew that Mary worked no miracles, preached no parables, nor left any legacy outside of her role as Christ's Mother. Yet even we understood that to be "most Mary-like" meant *be good*. Mary was sinless. She was fully human, yet she chose goodness. And now God calls us to do the same — to choose good and to resist evil.

As typically rambunctious youngsters, many of us were probably prevented from falling into more than menacing mischief by this gentle-yet-persistent prodding "to choose good and resist evil."

We were led to believe that with grace we could rise to holiness no matter our circumstances or shortfalls. And in a special way, we could look to Mary for prayer, strength, and support. I want my own children to look to Mary in the same way. I want them to know, too, that she is more than our Mother. She is a model for us to imitate in our climb to sainthood.

"Just think of what God did for us by giving us Mary. She is God's gift to us," I tell my kids. I doubt they've even begun to comprehend what I'm saying. How could they? I've only just begun to understand the concept myself!

When I told my curious then six-year-old son Michael, "God could have chosen any way he wished to come into the world instead of being born to Mary," he replied, "You mean he could have *just appeared like magic?*"

"In a way, yes. Remember, he was God. He didn't need a human mother or father. A savior could have just *appeared*. But God chose Mary to be his Mother, and when he was on the cross before he died and before he went back up to heaven, he asked Mary to be *our* Mother. Forever! Isn't that wonderful?"

One of my favorite Bible stories is the wedding feast at Cana because it demonstrates the tremendous power and influence of a mother. Mary tells Christ at the wedding celebration, "They have no wine" (John 2:3).

She does not nag, elaborate, or coax. She makes a simple statement. When our Lord responds by saying, "Woman, what concern is that to you and me? My hour has not yet come" (John 2:4), Mary ignores his initial refusal. Mary, like most mothers who live by intuition, would not take "no" for an answer. Instead, she instructs the waiters, "Do whatever he tells you" (John 2:5).

Mary had what we women like to call our "sixth sense." She *knew*, even when Christ claimed differently, that his hour had indeed come. Mary's prodding occasioned the first miracle and set her Son on the course of his public ministry.

How often as parents do we intuitively sense what is best for our children, our loved ones, or the people around us? And how often when we act on that perception do we, like Mary, though perhaps not totally aware, help perform little everyday miracles by serving the needs of others?

Our Blessed Mother teaches us at Cana to "press" for the miracles — in our own life and in those around us. And she urges us all to do whatever our Lord tells us.

Mary knew this was her Son's "hour." She knew it was time to begin his public ministry. By then she must have known, too, that her request of him to perform a public miracle would send him on the road to the persecution and destiny that Simeon and the Magi had predicted so many years earlier. And yet Mary, for the sake of her *other* children (you and me), prodded Christ to change the water into wine.

Mother Teresa of Calcutta, a Missionary of Charity, who spends herself caring for Christ's "poorest of the poor," says, "If you've ever *really* loved, then you know pain."

Mary, Christ's Mother, certainly knew pain and she, by her quiet consent to the will of God, demonstrates that the cross and love go together. They are both gifts from God. This "Cana love" — love for the good of another — is an example for all of us. Mary dedicated herself, body and soul, to become a virgin vessel for the honor and glory of God. And it was by the power of the Holy Spirit that she carried Christ to others.

So, too, each of us has been given a unique role to fulfill in God's divine plan. With prayer and grace we can become a vessel, carrying Christ in our daily deeds to others. When we do that, we begin to behave most "like Mary," offering each chore and challenge, every setback and test, as a gift of love to God.

In my own personal life, I can better scrub the floor, fold one more load of clothes, clean another dirty diaper, and wipe sticky fingerprints off the same old tired walls.

Okay. Let's talk "honesty" here, folks. There are probably more times when I moan and groan about my "lot in life" than those times of serenity when I "offer it up" with a smile and I carry up another load of laundry, or bathe one more bratty kid. I'm into *practice*, not *perfection*!

The older I grow, however, the more firmly convinced I remain that it is Mary who has the ear of Christ and pleads our cause. (And what a cause we parents have!) She *never* gives up on us. Even when it appears that we may be giving up! She's our Mother.

The Church reminds us that when we deliberately *live* Christ's life, we are then more "Mary-like." Each and every act, no matter how routine and insignificant, becomes a source for grace. Our soul, like Mary's, will begin to "proclaim the goodness of the Lord" to those around us.

Catholics may not have a corner on Mary, but we sure have a vantage point because traditionally and historically Marian devotion is not something new. Mary is a part of our faith and lives.

When I think of others, like my Protestant friend who is only beginning to discover the power of praying to Mary, I realize that there are millions more like her — perhaps right next door! That's worth a prayer all its own: "Lord, help me to be a good witness, giving honor and glory to you, and leading others to the feet of your Blessed Mother."

The late Bishop Fulton J. Sheen, respected and loved by Catholics and non-Catholics alike, had a great devotion to our Lady. In his many writings and lectures, especially when giving retreats to priests, he urged, "Go often to Mary; she is *your* Mother, too, and she has Christ's ear!"

* * *

A prayer that I frequently rely on for strength — most especially for those anxious times — is The Memorare:

Remember, O most gracious Virgin Mary, that never was it known that anyone who fled to your protection, implored your help, or sought your intercession was left unaided. Inspired with this confidence, I fly unto you, O Virgin of virgins, my Mother. To you I come, before you I stand, sinful and sorrowful. O Mother of the Word Incarnate, despise not my petitions, but in your mercy hear and answer me. Amen.

* * *

The Magnificat, or the Canticle of the Virgin Mary (Luke 1:47-55), offers inspiration and encouragement:

My soul magnifies the Lord,
and my spirit rejoices in God my Savior,
for he has looked with favor on the lowliness of his
  servant.
Surely, from now on all generations will call me
  blessed;

for the Mighty One has done great things for me,
and holy is his name.
His mercy is for those who fear him
from generation to generation.
He has shown strength with his arm;
he has scattered the proud in the thoughts of their
   hearts.
He has brought down the powerful from their thrones,
and lifted up the lowly;
he has filled the hungry with good things,
and sent the rich away empty.
He has helped his servant Israel,
in remembrance of his mercy,
according to the promise he made to our ancestors,
to Abraham and to his descendants forever.

* * *

A prayer that is traditionally said in the morning, at noon, and at sundown, and is appropriate at any hour of the day, is the Angelus:

V. The angel of the Lord declared unto Mary:
R. And she conceived of the Holy Spirit. *Hail Mary, etc.*
V. Behold the handmaid of the Lord:
R. Be it done unto me according to your word. *Hail Mary, etc.*
V. And the Word was made flesh:
R. And dwelt among us. *Hail Mary, etc.*
V. Pray for us, O holy Mother of God:
R. That we may be made worthy of the promises of Christ.

Let us pray:

Pour forth, we beseech you, O Lord, your grace into our hearts, that we, to whom the incarnation of Christ, your Son, was made known by the message of an angel, may, by his passion and cross, be brought to the glory of his resurrection. Through the same Christ, our Lord. Amen.

9

❦

The Rosary and Nighttime Prayers

I'll bet the Blessed Mother gets a kick out of some of the prayers said in her name.

Our Dominic, then four, was so anxious to be able to *lead* the family in our nightly Rosary, he practiced for days. Half the fun was showing up his older-yet-shyer brother Michael. When Dominic got to the Hail Mary, however, it sounded like our Lady was in the bakery business as he began with the words "Hail Mary, full of *glaze*. . ."

Now if you were the Blessed Mother, wouldn't you warm to a prayer like that? That's the way we figure it, too!

Oftentimes husbands and wives don't pray together, not because they don't want to, but because they are too timid or feel awkward in suggesting it. Most of us consider prayer and our faith as intensely personal.

Yet Catholics *know* that the sacrament of marriage has joined us as one, and this means a sharing of our physical, emotional, personal, and spiritual selves.

Having children can get us over the hump and should give us all the incentive we need to pray together. After all, our children's very souls are at stake, and teaching them how to pray can only be done if they see us doing it.

Personally speaking, as long as we have kids in the house, our family prayers will probably never be perfect. But they won't be dull either — and that's not always bad — especially when there are a few afraid-to-smile-someone-might-notice-me teens around.

But who couldn't smile at some of the prayer intentions we've heard? For example:

● God help get the baby out of Mom's stomach soon.

● Please tell the tooth fairy I swallowed it by accident and that it should still count!

● Dear Jesus, be sure to tell Santa we "gots" another kid!

● Help us find the missing frogs Dominic let loose! (Eeeeekkkk!)

If you haven't been doing it before, make yourself a promise that praying together before bedtime will be a *must* from now on. Never mind the wiggling tot, testy teen, or endless distractions. I know, I know. It's easier said than done. I'll be the first to admit there are days when even the thought of *prayer* has not kept me from wanting to get everyone cleaned up, bedded down, and out of sight.

Yet through the years we've come to see that something gentle and good occurs when we take a few moments at the end of each day to pray together as a family. We all come away a bit transformed and tranquil. And in a family our size and shape — that's something!

One of the things we've learned where children are involved is to expect *reverence* — but not *perfection*! So what if they're wiggly? So what if the phone is ringing, the toilet is still stopped up, or — worst-case scenario — "someone smells" (the one distraction that can't wait!)?

In that regard, we take solace in the words of St. Augustine who wrote that "the mere intent to pray is itself a prayer." In other words, God understands and is pleased by our effort.

Our children will pick up more by osmosis and example than any *feeling* of fervor they may occasionally experience. And the benefits are many, including nightly prayers together:

● Puts you and your young in a calm prayerful state — an end-of-the-day reminder of the many blessings to be thankful for, as well as others in need of our prayer. In fact, prayers become much more fervent if the children are given a chance to tell what special intentions they would like to pray about. We treat no intention as frivolous (especially frogs on the loose!).

● Going to bed with a prayer settles children down and gives them something sacred and reverent in their thoughts as one of the last events of their waking day — a sure prevention against restlessness or spooky or sinful thoughts.

● A golden opportunity for children to witness their

parents on their knees before God. If God is important in our lives, he will be also to our children.

● "Before bedtime prayer together" is a last-ditch opportunity to receive sanctifying grace — something we can always use more of.

● There's nothing more powerful than the Rosary. The Blessed Mother gave us the Rosary, a prayer that takes only ten to fifteen minutes to recite and is the most powerful prayer, outside of the Sacrifice of the Mass, that Catholics have in their spiritual arsenal.

An exaggeration? One of my friends, a convert to Catholicism from the Lutheran faith and a woman very knowledgeable and involved as a spiritual director in the charismatic community, says there are many non-Catholics who carry the rosary and say it in secret because they believe in its power. Can we do less?

Johnny and I worked the Rosary into our daily lives in gradual stages: We began with one decade, so as not to tire our little ones. After a while, when we felt the children could handle it, we graduated to two decades, then three, and ultimately the entire five decades. It has become a family staple in our home, and the protection it brings has rendered far more blessings than we'd ever dreamed possible.

Yes, we've experienced an occasional balker or "whiner" because it "takes too long." We began the practice when our children were young, however, and because our children know there is *no compromising* in areas of faith and morals, the objections were mild and few.

Quite frankly, I'm not running a popularity contest; nor am I going to poll the membership or manage this group by popular vote. I don't care if someone doesn't *like* saying the Rosary. I don't care if they think they can get more out of *talking to God* in the woods, in their room, or sitting in the lawn chair greased up with suntan oil and the radio blaring!

If they live under our roof (no matter the age), they'll be kneeling with us for nightly prayers (which is usually the Rosary). The alternative is spelled "suitcase." (This is what some would call "tough love.")

In fact, some of our more "mature" young adults, who were — shall we say — not always "enthusiastic" about the Rosary are today the same ones who offer their own intentions or give credit to the Rosary for special blessings and favors received. (Some miracles do take time! Thank you, Jesus.)

All in all, evening prayer is a faith-sharing and unifying experience. Just a few moments on our knees together in prayer can seem to lighten a load, relieve tensions, or temper areas of unrest and hurt.

In our home, John leads night prayers or the Rosary, announcing the decade. But the child who can name the Mystery for that decade gets to lead the family in prayer. This is one way to keep their attention and help them learn the Mysteries. Each Mystery is meant to encourage us to reflect on significant moments in the lives of Jesus and Mary. These events are rooted in Scripture and while our saying the Rosary may not have a noticeable positive effect — at first — I can guarantee that the blessings will *flow* with time.

On the nights we don't say the Rosary, our favorite evening prayer (which can also be said anytime throughout the day) is the one called Angel of God:

Angel of God, my guardian dear,
to whom God's love commits me here,
ever this day be at my side,
to light and guard, to rule and guide.
Amen.

* * *

For those of you who don't know (or have forgotten) how to pray the Rosary, here is how you do it (refer to the accompanying illustration [next page] as you read the following):

Begin with the Sign of the Cross: "In the name of the Father, and of the Son, and of the Holy Spirit. Amen." Then follow with the Apostles' Creed: "I believe in God, the Father Almighty, Creator of heaven and earth; and in Jesus Christ, his only Son, our Lord, who was conceived by the Holy Spirit, born of the Virgin Mary, suffered under Pontius Pilate, was crucified, died, and was buried. He descended into hell; the third day he rose again from the dead. He ascended into heaven and sits at the right hand of God, the Father Almighty; from thence he shall come to judge the living and the dead. I believe in the Holy Spirit, the holy Catholic Church,

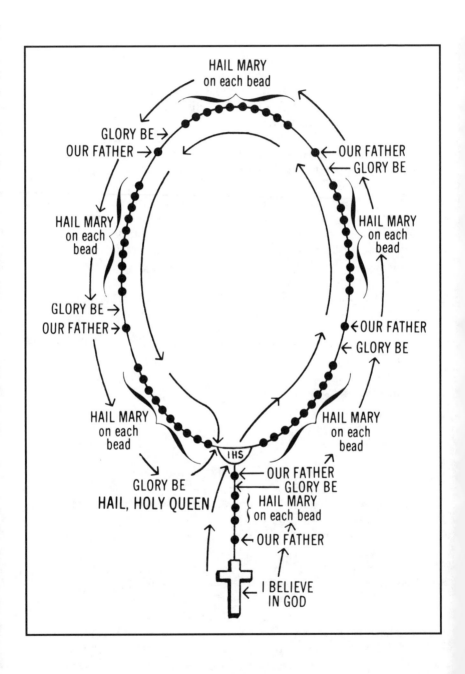

the communion of saints, the forgiveness of sins, the resurrection of the body, and life everlasting. Amen." Referring to the illustration, note where (that is, on which beads) the Our Father, the Hail Mary, the Glory Be (between beads), and Hail, Holy Queen should be recited (see below). It should also be noted that the appropriate Mystery is announced and briefly meditated on, following the recitation of the Hail Marys and Glory Be. For example, after the first three beads (Hail Marys) and Glory Be, you say, "The First Joyful Mystery: The Annunciation." This is followed by an Our Father, ten Hail Marys, a Glory Be, and the Second Joyful Mystery, and so on. As a general rule, the Joyful Mysteries are said on Monday and Thursday; the Sorrowful Mysteries on Tuesday and Friday; and the Glorious Mysteries on Wednesday and Saturday. Depending on the season, each of the Mysteries is recommended for Sunday.

● *Our Father:* "Our Father, who art in heaven, hallowed by thy name; thy kingdom come; thy will be done on earth as it is in heaven. Give us this day our daily bread; and forgive us our trespasses as we forgive those who trespass against us; and lead us not into temptation, but deliver us from evil. Amen."

● *Hail Mary:* "Hail Mary, full of grace. The Lord is with you. Blessed are you among women, and blessed is the fruit of your womb, Jesus. Holy Mary, Mother of God, pray for us sinners, now and at the hour of our death. Amen."

● *Glory Be to the Father:* "Glory be to the Father, and to the Son, and to the Holy Spirit. As it was in the beginning, is now, and ever shall be, world without end. Amen."

● *Hail, Holy Queen:* "Hail, holy Queen, Mother of Mercy! Hail, our life, our sweetness, and our hope! To you do we cry, poor banished children of Eve; to you do we send up our sighs, mourning and weeping in this vale of tears; turn, then, most gracious advocate, your eyes of mercy toward us; and after this, our exile, show unto us the blessed fruit of your womb, Jesus. O clement, O loving, O sweet Virgin Mary! [Pray for us, O holy Mother of God, that we may be made worthy of the promises of Christ.]"

Here are the Mysteries of the Rosary, along with some biblical references:

The Joyful Mysteries
1. The Annunciation (Luke 1:26-38).
2. The Visitation (Luke 1:39-47).
3. The Birth of Jesus (Matthew 1:18-25; Luke 2:1-7).
4. The Presentation of our Lord in the Temple (Luke 2:22-38).
5. The Finding of the Child Jesus in the Temple (Luke 2:41-52).

The Sorrowful Mysteries
1. The Agony in the Garden (Luke 22:39-46).
2. The Scourging at the Pillar (John 18:28-38).
3. The Crowning of Thorns (Mark 15:16-20).
4. The Carrying of the Cross (John 19:12-16).
5. The Crucifixion and Death of Our Lord (Matthew 27:33-56; Mark 15:22-41; John 19:16-30).

The Glorious Mysteries
1. The Resurrection (John 20).
2. The Ascension of Christ into Heaven (Luke 24:50-53).
3. The Descent of the Holy Spirit upon the Apostles (Acts 2:1-4).
4. The Assumption of the Blessed Mother into Heaven (Song of Solomon 2:8-14).
5. The Crowning of Mary, Queen of Heaven (Revelation 12:1-6).

10

❦

Saints' Appeal: One for Every Reason and Every Season

My kids, like most American youngsters, have their arsenals of stashed collectibles, valuables, and heroes. I'm not talking about the kind of collection we run across on most any given day in a big family. You know — the stale sandwich or encrusted ice-cream dish under the bed, the candy wrappers in drawers (never mind the waste basket just inches away), or the insect remains found hidden in with clean clothes. (Personally, the worst for me was the time Tina chose "mold" for her seventh-grade science project.)

My younger kids have little secret warehouses of stored "keepsakes" that could include almost *anything*. It might not look like much to us, but it means something special to them.

When our boys were young, it was sports figures and baseball trading cards, graduating to a few musical superstars in the teen years. With our girls, the attraction to television, film, and musical personalities begins early, and their bedroom, mirrors, and walls become littered with posters and photos of the ones who are currently "cool."

I haven't objected to most of the chosen "heroes" my kids have posted. In a couple of instances, when I knew more than they did about the personal life or offensive public behavior of a celebrity, the picture was removed from the wall. It may be their room, but I tell them, "We own the wall and it's part of our 'castle.' " It also speaks to those who enter our home, saying who we are and what we hold dear.

Most American kids today can readily tick off the names and achievements of their favorite sports, music, or screen idols. At age eight, our Michael, for example, could recite by heart the name and batting average of every Minnesota

Twins player. To say he was a fan is putting it mildly. He had stored over a thousand baseball cards under his bed, in his closet, or on his bookshelf — with a few of the more expensive ones in other hidden spots (out of his kid brothers' reach).

I'm not sure that's all bad. It's always good for children to have adult role models to look up to. It's up to us, as parents, however, to temper and channel that enthusiasm so that it remains healthy and in perspective. It's also up to us to discourage a fascination with heroes or celebrities who we may know to be immodest, indecent, or downright immoral. After all, our children *are* impressionable.

There's no doubt about it! Today's young people probably know more than they need to know about the world's celebrities. Yet even the best of Christian kids are little more than passingly familiar with the greatest heroes of all time — the saints!

Catholics are fortunate to have a stockpile of saintly heroes for "all occasions." But the only way our children are going to know about these remarkable individuals is if we become familiar with them first.

That began to happen at our house when I started reading the lives of the saints. I have several just for me. We also have numerous children's-style books and booklets featuring short narrations, colorful pictures, and easy-to-read stories.

It didn't take long to discover that saints are ordinary human beings like you and me but who did extraordinary things for the love of God. Most make for lively and fun reading.

Unfortunately there are those who misunderstand Catholic devotion to the saints and the Blessed Mother, mistakenly believing we are *worshiping* these men and women by our prayers. Not true.

Here's the way I explain it: If you felt the need for special prayers for a specific purpose or concern, wouldn't you call up your close friend and ask his or her prayerful support? And isn't it a wonderful consolation to know we have a friend praying for that special intention?

Well, we Catholics are merely doing the same, that is, asking other members of our spiritual family — the saints — to pray along with us. That is what is meant by the "communion of saints."

When our adopted son Tony graduated from high school, John and I gave him a prayer book and a small statue of St. Anthony, patron of lost articles.

Now Tony is an average fun-loving young man who almost gave his mild-mannered Polish father heart failure when he came home on his eighteenth birthday wearing an earring in one ear. Yet this same independent-minded young adult believes he has an "in" with his namesake, St. Anthony.

One day, upon returning after taking his driving test (for the second time), he confided, "I told him, 'All right, Anthony. I could use your help here. If it's God's will that I pass my test, I'd sure appreciate it. If not — welllll — I'll just keep trying.' "

Tony's casual prayer was nonetheless sincere. And God knew it. (Incidentally, Tony did pass that second time.)

Christians who ignore the angels and saints cheat themselves out of a most powerful source of prayer. Johnny and I purposely chose biblical, saints', or derivatives of saints' names for our thirteen children. We want them, like Tony, to feel a special spiritual kinship to their particular heavenly hero and to turn to that saint often in prayer.

As for the angels, we tell our children, "When God placed you in our care, Dad and I had you baptized just as soon as we could. We promised God *for* you, until you are old enough to promise for yourself. Baptism makes you for the first time a member of the Body of Christ. Then God assigns you your very own guardian angel who is here just for you. This angel will never let you stray too long, or allow you to get too far away from God's love, as long as you are faithful."

It is important for children to be aware of their own personal guardian angel who stands at their side ready to offer prayers, protection from harm, and an inspiration to do good.

In addition to our own personal angel, there is another angel we can call on: St. Michael the Archangel, who is said to be God's most powerful warrior. He can bring us through times of great fear, imminent danger, or simply to relieve an anxious heart. He can be both fortifying and comforting, and the prayer to him is one every Catholic would do well to learn: "St. Michael the Archangel, defend us in battle; be our defense against the wickedness and snares of the devil. May God rebuke him, we humbly pray; and do you, O Prince of the heavenly host, by the power of God, cast into hell Satan and all the other evil spirits who prowl about the world seeking the ruin of souls. Amen."

St. Joseph, foster father of Jesus, is best known as the patron of fathers and protector of the family. He also is the saint many turn to for help with vocation, employment, or housing decisions. In fact, many Catholics wouldn't think of building (Joseph was a carpenter), buying, or selling a home, without praying to St. Joseph for guidance and help. My Johnny claims he has run to Joseph when our financial needs were greater than his paycheck. (Thank you, St. Joseph!)

Personally, I don't take the financial problems as seriously as I do kids with problems or problem kids. I do know, however, that when Johnny faced serious surgery for what turned out to be a benign tumor on the brain, it was Joseph we turned to in prayer.

More recently, when our college-age Tim had to make a decision about job choices, I told him Joseph was his man. He's a strong and family-oriented saint that all boys and men can rely on in prayer. There are many devotionals to St. Joseph, including this one: "We come to you, O blessed Joseph, in our sore distress. Having sought the aid of your most blessed spouse, we now confidently implore your assistance also. We humbly beg, that mindful of the dutiful affection that bound you to the immaculate Virgin Mother of God, and of the fatherly love with which you cherished the Child Jesus, you will lovingly watch over the heritage that Jesus Christ purchased with his blood, and by your powerful intercession help us in our urgent need. Most powerful guardian of the Holy Family, protect the chosen race of Jesus Christ; drive far from us, most loving father, every pest of error and corrupting sin. From your place in heaven, most powerful protector, graciously come to our aid in this conflict with the powers of darkness, and as you delivered the Child Jesus from the supreme peril of life, so now we ask you to defend the holy Church of God from the snares of her enemies and from all adversity. Have each of us always in your keeping, that, following your example, and borne up by your strength, we may be able to live holy, die happily, and so enter the everlasting bliss of heaven. Amen."

One of my best spiritual friends is a saint who died a Carmelite nun at age twenty-four and became known and loved throughout the world after her death. She is often referred to as the "greatest saint in modern times" because she lived a simple and very humble life, yet offered up every task and undertaking as a prayer, calling it her "little way" to God.

Over the years, when I've had something most pressing on my mind, I have gone to St. Thérèse of Lisieux (also known as Thérèse of the Child Jesus and Thérèse the Little Flower) for prayers and support. And I have never been disappointed. Even when things don't turn out as I planned, she's helped me see the *miracles* in my life and in the lives of others.

In the early years I admit I used St. Thérèse most when praying for a new baby. Believe it or not, we did spend time discussing and praying about adding "another" to our crew! I think most people figure we just got married, walked back down the aisle, and *Abracadabra* — an instant family of fifteen appeared!

The more I prayed to Thérèse, and read books by her and about her, the closer I felt to her. In the end, I credit this invisible friend for many answered prayers. She is one of the primary reasons I became a Third Order Carmelite.

Thérèse devoted her life and her physical illness and suffering for priests and vocations to the priesthood. She also had a great devotion to good Catholic family life and, in fact, it was because of her own devout parents and upbringing that she was drawn to the religious life. A great prayer partner to call upon, in my book!

St. Thérèse promises that when you say a novena to her she will send a sign of roses (be it the fragrance of a rose or a real or artificial rose). The novena is to be said on five consecutive days (before eleven in the morning if possible), along with five Hail Marys, five Our Fathers, and five Glory Be's.

Here is a little prayer to St. Thérèse that you might want to say now and then: "St. Thérèse the Little Flower, please pick me a rose from the heavenly garden and send it to me with a message of love. Ask God to grant the favor I implore and tell him I will love him daily more and more. Amen."

Another heavenly friend is St. Anthony of Padua. Best known as the patron saint of lost articles, Anthony was a priest and Doctor of the Church who lived in the thirteenth century. Even during his lifetime he was regarded as a legendary hero because of the remarkable miracles attributed to him. It was the return of a stolen sacred book of psalms, according to one account, that gave Anthony his reputation of finding missing items.

I've turned to St. Anthony for help in finding everything from a misplaced bankbook to a parking spot. Now I know there are skeptics who say we're not supposed to "bother God or his saints" with these little irritants in life; but the way I figure it, God wants to be included in each and every act of our waking day, and either those little irritants will become a source for holiness if used as an opportunity for prayer, or they could become occasions of sin by our ill temper or impatience.

I'll stick with St. Anthony. When I *don't* get the parking spot or things don't turn out *my* way, I know, too, that just saying a "Praise the Lord, anyway" is far more beneficial than grumbling through gritted teeth. It sure doesn't hurt either for our kids to see us in prayer for the "little everyday things."

St. Anthony is the saintly friend I go to for lost articles or "straying" children. And it works! A simple Our Father, Hail Mary, Glory Be, or personal salutation to St. Anthony is enough of a prayer to get him working for whatever it is we need.

Our daughter Chrissy loves the prayer of St. Francis of Assisi. I can still remember her enthusiasm as a young third grader the day she bounded in the door after school.

"Oh, Mommy!" she exclaimed excitedly. "We learned the most beautiful song in school today, and when you come to our First Friday Mass, you'll get to hear us sing it. I can hardly wait for you to come. We've been practicing it all week, and the words are so beautiful. It was written by this guy that's now a saint. He loved all the animals and birds, and his name is Francis."

Through her growing-up years, the Song of St. Francis remained Chrissy's favorite. And because of that song, she felt a kinship and wanted to know more about the saint who inspired it.

Chrissy is now grown and married. But guess which song she and her husband, Andy, chose to be sung at Communion time on their wedding day? That's right — the Prayer of St. Francis, which goes like this:

Lord, make me an instrument of your peace.
Where there is hatred, let me sow love;
where there is injury, pardon;
where there is discord, unity;
where there is doubt, faith;
where there is despair, hope;
where there is darkness, light;
where there is sadness, joy.
O Divine Master,
grant that I may not so much seek
to be consoled as to console;
to be understood as to understand;
to be loved as to love.
For it is in giving that we receive;
it is in pardoning that we are pardoned;
and it is in dying that we are born to eternal life.
Amen.

* * *

What's really remarkable about the saints is that each one has a special area and mission. I've turned to St. Gerard Majella, patron of pregnant women, when we were expecting our babies (even the adopted ones). I've prayed for my school-age youngsters with the help of St. John Bosco, known as the apostle of youth, who spent his life caring for young boys and girls. St. Martin de Porres became a family favorite when our son Charlie (who is black/Cambodian) arrived at the age of five and a half from an orphanage in Vietnam wearing a huge crucifix tied to a string around his neck with a Martin de Porres medal attached.

As a mother of many, I've taken solace from St. Anne (the mother of Mary) who raised a sinless child to become the Mother of God. (Here's a mother I want to keep in touch with!) For my children I've turned to St. Catherine of Siena, who was the twenty-fifth child in a poor family but became known as one of the finest theological minds and a Doctor of the Church. The question I keep asking is, "Where did she find a corner to pray?"

I'm still learning about St. Teresa of Ávila (a reformer and mystic), as well as St. Francis de Sales, St. Charles Borromeo, St. Maximilian Kolbe, and Edith Stein (a Jew who converted and became a Carmelite). Both Kolbe and Stein died for their faith during the Nazi holocaust. All were prolific writers for the honor and glory of God.

There are hosts of others in our spiritual arsenal including St. Jude Thaddeus (patron saint of "lost causes"), St. Frances Cabrini (who became the first United States citizen to be canonized), and Kateri Tekawitha, the first native American to be raised to the status of Blessed.

Once you begin reading about the lives of the saints, you will find your own army of extraordinary people who did — and continue to do — extraordinary things for the love of God.

11

❧

Saints Alive

If you're like me, you probably don't feel much like a saint, yet St. Paul repeatedly wrote that even on earth we were all to be Christ's "living saints."

We can all readily point to the obvious "greats" who go about their daily lives, almost routinely performing corporal works of mercy. Mother Teresa, the Missionary of Charity nun who devoted her life to caring for the "poorest of the poor," is perhaps the best-known spiritual giant of our times. Yet each of us can think of other corporal "workers" of mercy who give of their time, talent, and tenacity for the love of God and neighbor.

Two modern missionary-types that come to my mind are Rosemary Taylor (an Australian social worker) and Wende Grant (her American counterpart), both of whom dedicated themselves tirelessly to the orphans and needy of Southeast Asia, particularly Vietnam. Were it not for these two, and those who worked along with them, Charlie and Tony (our two adopted sons from that part of the world) and over one thousand other youngsters would most likely not be alive and thriving today.

The story of these two angels of mercy is worth sharing.

During the years 1967 to 1975, Taylor worked in Vietnam, offering medical, emotional, and/or financial support to help keep struggling families intact. As the Vietnam war worsened, the orphans kept coming. Ultimately, she and Grant helped to place 1,132 children for adoption, hundreds of whom were taken in by U.S. families.

Among the children these caring women saved were babies left in hospital nurseries where poor mothers were bunched three to a single bed; babies stashed in doorways; babies dropped off at Catholic churches and police stations; babies put in dumpsters. Fortunately, desperate but caring relatives, friends, and neighbors — overwhelmed by deteriorating conditions brought on by the war — found ways to deliver many of the babies and young children to individuals like Wende Grant and Rosemary Taylor.

Rosemary Taylor's book *Orphans of War* poignantly tells of the hundreds of infants who were too small, too sickly, or "unstimulated" (unloved), and whose only legacy was a cardboard box in an unmarked grave behind the orphanage courtyard. In Vietnam, as many as eighty percent of those war orphans under a year of age died.

Our Tony — who, as pointed out earlier, arrived on a special medical visa at the age of two months, weighing in at five pounds, and diagnosed with severe malnutrition, starvation diarrhea, and dehydration — would have been one of those death statistics. Not from disease or disability, but from lack of love and bonding.

Taylor and her crew valiantly vowed to handle, hold, and hug each and every child who came their way. In those cases where their efforts failed, they tearfully saw that each little one received a name and a dignified burial.

Ignoring the hysteria and war around her, Taylor set up classrooms and tutors for the older youngsters, with individual and group activity for preschoolers. She demanded that none of her charges be fed by bottle propping — a method used in overcrowded hospitals and other institutions for infants who were identified as "illegitimate" and unwanted. Such a method often caused death by drowning as the overused nipple tore and burst, and the unattended infant choked on the gushing formula.

Wende Grant became Taylor's American collaborator by forming Friends For All Children, a group that offered medical and financial support, later becoming the primary conduit for the U.S. adoption effort. Grant did more than process papers and cut bureaucratic red tape in order to bring children and adoptive parents together. She organized and galvanized crews of caring individuals across America who responded to the Vietnamese children and families, by collecting, packing, and shipping thousands of pounds of food, clothing, and urgently needed medical supplies.

In Vietnam, Taylor challenged a culture immobilized by conflict. She faced a bureaucracy of endless paperwork, red tape, visa requirements, and waiting lists, refusing to ignore the poverty, disease, supply shortages, fleeing families, and the stockpiling of orphans that became the status quo. Neither the primitive working conditions and governmental balking nor the hostility toward illegitimate children and/or adoption efforts by both Asian and Western sources diminished her dogged determination to care, cure, and save — no matter the odds.

The tenacity of Taylor along with her fierce devotion to her children is demonstrated most eloquently by her courageous departure after her eight years of effort in Vietnam. In spite of repeated warnings, she refused to leave. By 1975 she had four orphanage houses bursting with six hundred infants and small children, many with limbs missing, and countless others who were victims of polio, blindness, and other severe physical and/or mental disabilities.

Two of our children were caught in that quagmire. One, Daniel Thanh, a seven-year-old victim of polio whom we had already legally adopted, was stranded in a Vietnamese hospital awaiting visa approval. We had nervously waited nearly a year for his arrival, yet each time he was scheduled to leave, he was "bumped" off because of medical and/or visa regulations.

Eventually, a C5A Air Force jet attempted to airlift the last remaining orphans out before Saigon's fall to Communism. Mechanical problems caused the plane to crash in a rice field shortly after takeoff. Most of the crew, orphanage workers, and young passengers were killed. Our Daniel was among them, and so the hopes and plans we had for him became nothing more than dreams.

In spite of the tragedies and ensuing danger, Rosemary Taylor relentlessly insisted that every last child be seen to safety before she would leave Vietnam. And she did. Only then did she consent to a last-minute escape by crawling over the American Embassy barbed-wire wall where she was airlifted from the Embassy roof by helicopter to a naval cargo ship already bulging with 4,551 evacuees.

Because of her persistence, several hundred orphaned children, including a young black-skinned Cambodian youngster of five and one-half, escaped and were safely escorted to the island of Guam (a U.S. territory) for evacuation and medical care. Upon recovery, this little lad was later airlifted to America to become by adoption a Kuharski.

We are indebted to Rosemary Taylor, who made it all possible. She brushes off such heroic stubbornness by quoting Psalm 84:

The sparrow has found its home at last;
The swallow a nest for its young.

* * *

Her stubbornness along with her unflinching belief in the uniqueness and value of each and every human being, in each individual's wantedness and worth, no matter the age, race, or condition, became the motivating force that drove her and her helpers to continue to freely give of themselves even in the face of disease and death. It is only because of this humble Australian woman, and her corps of committed volunteers, that thousands of youngsters, like ours, are alive and loved today.

Recognized after the war for her valor, Taylor was awarded the "Member of the Order of Australia" decoration by her homeland.

Perhaps more startling than her eight-year effort in Vietnam, which ended with the fall of Saigon to Communism and her narrow escape to safety, is the fact that at this writing she can be found not on a luxury liner or "extended" holiday, but in Bangkok where she struggles against famine, disease, homelessness, and hopelessness. Rosemary Taylor is again busy offering love and security to God's most forgotten — the world's orphaned children. If that's not an example of corporal works of mercy in action, I don't know what is.

DOROTHY AND MIKE

As remarkable as Rosemary and those who serve in far-off mission areas are, most of us know of individuals right next door who are leading Christlike on-the-road-to-sainthood lives by their example to others. Mike and Dorothy Fleming are two individuals who readily come to mind.

They claim it was an easy decision to move Dorothy's sickly mother into their home. "It's the right thing to do for your mother and one that should receive no notice or applause,"

Dorothy says. In less than six months, her eighty-four-year-old mother experienced two major surgeries and three hospitalizations because of a fractured hip. Such confinements were the first — outside of giving birth — for this once vital and vibrant mother of three. The afflictions, coupled with progressive dementia, left Dorothy's mom dependent upon wheelchair, walker, and twenty-four-hour care.

Dorothy's goal was to see to it that whatever time remains, her mother will feel the love and closeness of family. Easier said than done.

Bringing Grandma home means no more family workroom for Mike and Dorothy. And for six-year-old Catherine, it means a sharing of bedroom and play area. So it's "Move over, make-believe kitchen set, dollhouse, Barbies, and furry friends and make room for a Porta Potti, walker, 'gerry' chair, wheelchair, clothes, and 'meds.' "

The decision means that Dorothy is responsible for her mother's day-to-day care. No easy task. Grandma is one of those middle-of-the-night roamers, with wakings and bathroom visits occurring as frequently as every two hours.

It means also that there will be no more daylong outings to the zoo, no overnight trips — not even a Saturday evening dinner with that "coupon special," without first arranging to have someone there for Grandma.

A simple visit to the doctor with Grandma may take all morning and part of the afternoon. Just bathing, dressing, coaxing, and calming any undue fears on her part takes time. And then there is the challenge of bundling for the sub-zero temperatures, not to mention waiting for Project Mobility to arrive, and getting Grandma to and from, as well as in and out, for the scheduled visit. "It's teaching me patience," Dorothy states matter-of-factly.

To the outside observer like myself, the phrase "Doing for the sake of another" readily comes to mind. The hardest part is not the inconvenience, interrupted sleep, or the frequent accidents and messes caused by a not-always-controlled urinary and bowel system. No. The hardest part is the caring — *for who knows how long.*

Much of the time Dorothy's mom forgets where she is or who she's with. "She looks and talks just like my daughter,

Dorothy. But my daughter's too busy with her family. I don't see much of her," Dorothy's mother once confided to me during a visit. Always careful not to embarrass her, Dorothy just smiled and sat by her side stroking her gnarled and weathered hand.

It takes a special grace to serve someone who doesn't even know what sacrifices are being made on his or her behalf. "We're doing what Jesus would do," is Dorothy's quick response.

No slight is intended to those who choose nursing home or institutional care for a dependent loved one. Any health-care professional working in a nursing home can readily tick off the names of the patients who are most coddled and loved by family members. When done in love, the decision to place a loved one in out-of-home care creates great demands on adult children. It means frequent visits, altered family schedules, holidays with conflicts, and a constant presence and involvement in an area that tugs, with each decision and visit, at the heartstrings and emotions of everyone involved.

A decision to remove a loved one from the privacy of home and familiar surroundings, and to watch the loved one attempt to adjust to a strange institutional setting, with rotating staff and caregivers, unfamiliar roommates, and unusual sounds and smells — such a decision brings about a sense of sadness and loss all its own.

Yet for those offering at-home care the commitment and work are not nearly as difficult as the confinement and social restriction. Grandma's not the only shut-in. It's also Dorothy and Mike and the thousands of others who willingly put their lives on hold in order to care for a loved one.

It is these citizens among us who provide a most valuable witness. They demonstrate an unconditional — an "even when you're sick and time-consuming" — love. It's the kind of love that makes the command "Honor your father and your mother" come to mind, and come to life. In my view, this is pro-life in the trenches at its best.

VICKEY AND CHET

Vickey and Chet were a newly married couple who responded with love when Vickey's dying mother asked before her death if they would look after Vickey's sickly brother.

That was more than forty years ago and, aside from one four-day vacation on which the two went by themselves, Vickey and Chet have cared for brother Fritz in their home ever since. They still managed to raise two children and one foster daughter and, now that their children are grown and married, they generously serve as baby-sitters for their grandchildren. In addition, Vickey took time to work on various church committees and to serve as president of her parish Council of Catholic Women.

Fritz, now in his seventies, has become more fragile and his needs more serious, and although Vickey and Chet are in their sixties, he remains secure in their care.

There must be occasions when Vickey and Chet feel penned in or frustrated by their circumstances. Perhaps they've even vocalized their impatience. Yet they continue to lovingly care for Fritz, for their children, for their grandchildren, and for others within their church and community. Truly they are saints unheralded!

TED AND CAROL

A young couple named Ted and Carol rushed up to visit with Johnny and me during a pro-life prayer gathering. The two were eager for us to see the newest addition to their family. In the arms of the young mother was a delicate baby girl.

Carol gushed, "We want you to meet our Emily. She's our recent adoption and she's doing quite well after the recent heart surgery she underwent. We're so thrilled to have her."

Many would have perceived little Emily, a Down's syndrome baby, as someone who would require special attention and assistance throughout her life. Ted and Carol, on the other hand, saw her adoption as an opportunity to love. Christians in action and sainthood in the making, by my measure!

Sometimes the hardest course to follow, yet the quickest path to sainthood, is not to go to a far-off mission but rather to work with those in our midst: perhaps a family member or someone within our community who is "hungry" for love and affection.

Truly, it is these kinds of individuals and their commitment to Christ that we can look to as examples and role models for us and our children. Ordinary people doing extraordinary things for the love of God. The not-so-well-known saints among us deserve our encouragement and prayers.

12

❦

Advent Angels and Co-Redeemers

Our Advent took on a deeper meaning the year our Mary Elizabeth, then eight, came home from school excitedly describing her Advent task. The students drew names from their class to be the other's "Advent angel" for the remaining days before Christmas.

What a wonderful way to get young people to be concerned about another's needs. Instead of centering the coming of Christmas on self, this little exercise drew the children out-ward — to the blessings that their prayers and little offer-ings could be in another child's life. The tradition of exchanging Advent angels has since become an annual ac-tivity at the Kuharski household.

On the first Sunday of Advent our children draw one another's names and spend the four weeks before Christmas doing little acts of kindness for the person whose name they drew. Perhaps it's straightening the "drawee's" room when he or she is not home, doing that person's chores (dishes, dusting, etc.), or writing little prayer notes to be left with a little piece of candy under the "drawee's" pillow.

Even our teens and young adults participate and look for-ward to the event, especially the drawing of names and the eventual surprise of knowing the identity of their "angel."

Of course, there are always a few rolled eyes, sighs of "Not her!" or "Oh, no, he's such a nerd!" as they unwrap the names and realize they are committed to four weeks of pampering a sister or brother who normally drives them up the wall. But that's part of the fun!

The first year our Charlie moved away to college he called home at Advent time to ask if we'd picked names. When we assured him it was Advent-as-usual, he responded, "Gee, I feel left out this year."

The season of Lent is another opportunity for faith-building. Not only can parents promote the value of sacrifice in their children but they also know that the sheer discipline of kids depriving themselves (most especially our young who have *so much*) helps build character and self-control. We modern-day moms and dads can always use a refresher course in that area as well.

When Lent comes around, Johnny and I talk to our kids about what things we're giving up. They all know that my addictions are popcorn (almost every evening!), coffee, and chocolate candy. When I tell them then that these are the things I'm giving up for Lent, they know it means *sacrifice*! And since most kids don't want to be outdone in commitment and endurance, they will eagerly rise to the challenge of penitential giving.

Acts of mercy and charity are also excellent character-builders to practice during Advent or Lent. Visiting the sick, grocery shopping for someone elderly or a shut-in, shoveling or raking another's yard without expecting financial payment are little ways of letting others see the love of God.

A Lenten denial that has become a Kuharski "annual" is to give up television, except for the evening news or special programs. Steeling ourselves against the initial complaints the first few years, we discovered a hidden reward — we spent more time in play with one another. The older kids took time to read to the younger ones, and we all had more time to talk, listen, or play cards or board games with one another.

Forgoing TV is now a Lenten *must*. Of course, some of our teens and young adults accuse us of "forcing" such a denial on them, and my usual response is, "You don't have to give up television. You can watch it all you want. You just can't watch it at our house because this house gave it up."

In addition to self-denial during this time of preparation for Easter, we urge our children to go to confession frequently and to attend Mass during the week if at all possible.

"If the devil thinks we're working hard to get closer to God, he's going to do all he can to bust it up," I've warned my young. "Attending Mass during Advent and Lent and going frequently to confession gives us even more grace to fight off the temptations thrown our way."

As elementary as it may seem, putting a philosophy of love into practice is "easier said than done." Practically speaking, many of us have no problem loving the Russians, the Arabs, the homeless, or the rejected. It's that alcoholic relative that "tension-fills" our holiday gatherings; it's that moody and unpredictable teen, the "temper-tantrummed" toddler, demanding employer, impossible-to-love neighbor, or that unappreciative mate who tests our endurance, challenges our charity, and taunts our saintliness.

David Porter in his book *Mother Teresa, the Early Years* describes what may be the hidden secret of her inner strength. He tells of a Belgian woman named Jacqueline de-Decker, who because of deteriorating health, a number of spinal operations, and the need to convalesce, was unable to fulfill the missionary work in India she once thought was her vocation. Instead, after meeting Mother Teresa, she and the prayer-dependent nun determined that deDecker's "call" was to offer up her life of suffering and pain for the Missionaries of Charity effort.

So valuable does Mother Teresa see such a partnership of prayer and sacrifice that she wrote to deDecker in 1952, "The work here is tremendous and needs workers, it is true, but I need souls like yours to pray and suffer for the work. . . ."

This relationship became a central part of the Missionaries of Charity and, in 1953, when the first ten novices were about to take their vows, Mother Teresa felt each one should have a "spiritual link" with someone who was sick or suffering. Jacqueline deDecker, in response, found people in Europe willing to take on that commitment.

Nowadays "there are about 2,000 Sick and Suffering Co-Workers (silent partners) who have accepted the demanding call to love and serve Jesus not for what He gives but for what He takes," according to Porter.

Our own "call" may not demand a lifetime commitment to the work of a faraway mission. Instead, we may be called, as was St. Thérèse of Lisieux (the "Little Flower"), to offer daily each mundane and hardly noticeable task, injury, or adversity for the salvation of others. St. Thérèse called this her "little way" in which every interruption or irritation became an "opportunity to offer."

Many Catholics today still remember from their own youth the advice of their teachers, parents, and grandparents to "offer it up" when one suffers some injury or disappointment.

Putting such advice into practice may mean that an office worker or clerk humbly accepts the thoughtless or rude remark of a co-worker or customer, resisting the urge to strike back. The teenage child sees household chores or homework as opportunities rather than oppression. Moms and dads look at the mounds of laundry, "fix-it" tasks, demanding schedules, or lack of "time for just me" as a "call" to sacrifice. (No fair complaining.) The elderly, the sick, and the handicapped can give to God their arthritis, bursitis, or other frustrating limitations.

And who could be the beneficiaries of such little offerings? We could begin with our own family members, parish priests, and friends; the alcoholic relative who makes our holiday gatherings so tense, the moody teen, the selfish spouse; or even the local abortionist or a pro-abortion politician. Whether it's someone easy to love or impossible to like, all of us (the unbelievers most of all) need a spiritual hug. And that's really the essence of an "Advent angel" — creating opportunities to offer that spiritual hug!

13

❧

Prayers for All Occasions

St. Paul repeatedly reminds us in his epistles to "pray always" and to "do everything in prayer." When I first read his words, I'd think to myself, "I'll bet he never had to contend with a houseful of kids. Let him wake up to the sound of a dozen eggs dropped on a newly washed kitchen floor, get a notice of 'head lice' sent home the same day out-of-town company is arriving, or nurse a houseful of tots with the twenty-four-hour flu. Then we'll see how practical it is to 'pray always.' "

"Praying always" sounds good in theory, but — let's face it — how realistic is it? Well, I'm here to say that once I began to put prayer into practice (I'm still working on it), the more I understand St. Paul's instruction. Praying and thanking God for *all* the circumstances of the day has a way of uplifting and encouraging us. It's like singing when you're down. In addition, we are setting a good example for our children and inspiring them to do the same. After all, most of us parents realize early on in our parenting years that our children learn far more by imitation than instruction.

We can praise God in *all* things by turning every event, every happening, including the unhappy or unpleasant, to God. Yes, it's a little hard to thank God for the bad news as well as the good. But once you get into the habit, it becomes easy.

My kids are now used to hearing me whisper a "Thank you, Jesus" or "Praise God" for the ups as well as the downs of daily life. Granted, I may say it through clenched teeth when it's a fender-bender accident, a houseful of kids passing around the twenty-four-hour flu (yuk!), or some unexpected "tragedy" — like having all of the children home from school with a day off when I had plans for lunch.

Yet something happens when you turn an unpleasant situation over to God with praise. Just being thankful "in all things" reminds us that we are God's children and that we refuse to be held hostage or frustrated by any catastrophe that Satan throws our way.

The late Bishop Fulton J. Sheen, a prolific author and speaker, used to say, "When I drive by a hospital I always feel a certain sadness knowing that so many lie there sick and in pain. All that suffering is going to waste if they're not offering it up to God."

Bishop Sheen constantly encouraged believers to view every occurrence of the day — most especially the illnesses and adversities — as opportunities to become co-redeemers with Christ by offering up their joys and sufferings for the love of God and the benefit of others.

My kids hear me say it often. When my Tina complained of an upcoming exam, I said, "Offer it up." So, too, when Theresa complains about washing the kitchen floor. And when Angela lay on the hospital operating table, so little and so frightened, before her emergency appendectomy, I reminded her, "Don't let all that suffering go to waste, Angie. Offer it up."

And she did. My greatest reward was hearing her several weeks later consolingly instruct a younger brother to "offer up" his scraped knee when he came running in the door for a Band-Aid and some tender loving care.

With regard to prayer, the Sacrifice of the Mass is the highest form of prayer, and the Eucharist is the reception of Christ himself. No prayer can top that.

We can, however, make our whole day a prayer and offering to God, if we offer each action and every activity, no matter how trivial, to God. A real walking "head-to-toe Alleluia," which is what St. Augustine says every Christian ought to be!

Where children are involved, it's important to remember:

✔ **The key is flexibility, not rigid rules.** Most of us learned early on in our parenting to be flexible and not to expect perfection. Passing on the faith to our young or teaching them how to pray occurs in our homes and hearts over a lifetime. Prayer is a conversation with God. He *knows* there are going to be occasions when our prayer time is less than perfect or shortchanged because of pressures. Remember what St. Augustine says: "The mere intent to pray" is a form of prayer if we want it to be so.

✔ **If you've never before prayed with your spouse or youngsters, begin today**. Invite your children to pray before meals, bedtime, or *anytime* with a simple invitation: "Let's just stop and say a little prayer to God." If some refuse — all the more reason for *you* to pray! If prayer has not previously been a part of your routine, you might simply explain to your children, "Dad and I let our lives get too busy. We didn't mean to leave God out; we just got away from talking to him as often as we should. But we're going to change that — starting *right now*, and we'd like you to help us!"

✔ **The best prayer of all is the one that comes from the heart!** Many beautiful prayers have been written to help us pray. The one prayer God loves best, however, is the one we express in our own words, unpolished as it is, to him.

✔ **As parents we are the primary educators of our young.** The Church teaches that we have the Holy Spirit to guide us and the Blessed Mother in our corner. So what are we waiting for? Let's not waste a minute!

Here are some prayers that are staples of the Catholic faith:

ACT OF FAITH ✝ O my God, I firmly believe that you are one God in three divine Persons, Father, Son, and Holy Spirit. I believe that your divine Son became man and died for our sins, and that he will come again to judge the living and the dead. I believe these and all the truths that the holy Catholic Church teaches because you have revealed them who can neither deceive nor be deceived. Amen.

ACT OF HOPE ✝ O my God, relying on your infinite mercy and promises, I hope to obtain pardon of my sins, the help of your grace, and life everlasting, through the merits of Jesus Christ, my Lord and Redeemer. Amen.

ACT OF LOVE ✝ O my God, I love you above all things with my whole heart and soul because you are all-good and worthy of all my love. I love my neighbor as myself for the love of you. I forgive all who have injured me and ask pardon of all whom I have injured. Amen.

BEFORE AN OPERATION ✝ Loving Father, I entrust myself to your care this day. Guide with wisdom and skill the minds and hands of those who minister in your name, and grant that every cause of illness be removed, that I may be restored to soundness of health and learn to live in more perfect harmony with you and with my fellowman, through Jesus Christ. Into your hands I commend my body and soul. Amen.

PRAYER FOR VOCATIONS ✝ O Lord our God, you established the Church as a sign of your continuing presence in the world. We ask you to raise up faithful ministers to your Church in the priesthood and religious life so that the message of faith, justice, and love contained in the gospel may be brought into the hearts of all people. We ask this through Christ, our Lord. Amen.

PARENTS' PRAYER ✝ Most loving Father, the perfect example of parenthood, you have entrusted our children to us to bring them up for you and prepare them for everlasting life. Assist us with your grace so that we may fulfill this sacred duty with competence and love. Teach us what to give and what to withhold. Show us when to reprove, when to praise, and when to be silent. Make us gentle and considerate, yet firm and watchful. Keep us from the weakness of indulgence and the excess of severity. Give us the courage to be disliked sometimes by our children, when we must do necessary things that are displeasing in their eyes. Give us the imagination to enter their world in order to understand and guide them. Grant us all the virtues we need to lead them by word and example in the ways of wisdom and piety. One day, with them, may we enter into the joys of our true and lasting home with you in heaven. Amen.

SPIRITUAL COMMUNION ✝ *When unable to receive Holy Communion, it is a pious practice to make a Spiritual Com-*

munion. Say the following prayer of St. Francis: I believe that you, O Jesus, are in the most holy sacrament. I love you and desire you. Come into my heart. I embrace you. Oh, never leave me. May the burning and most sweet power of your love, O Lord Jesus Christ, I beseech you, absorb my mind, that I may die through love of your love, who were graciously pleased to die through love of my love. Amen.

The above prayers just scratch the surface. There are many great prayers and litanies of the Church offered to our Lord, his Blessed Mother, and the saints. However, the prayer our heavenly Father loves most to hear, as I said earlier, is the simple one we utter, unpolished and simple, that comes straight from the heart.

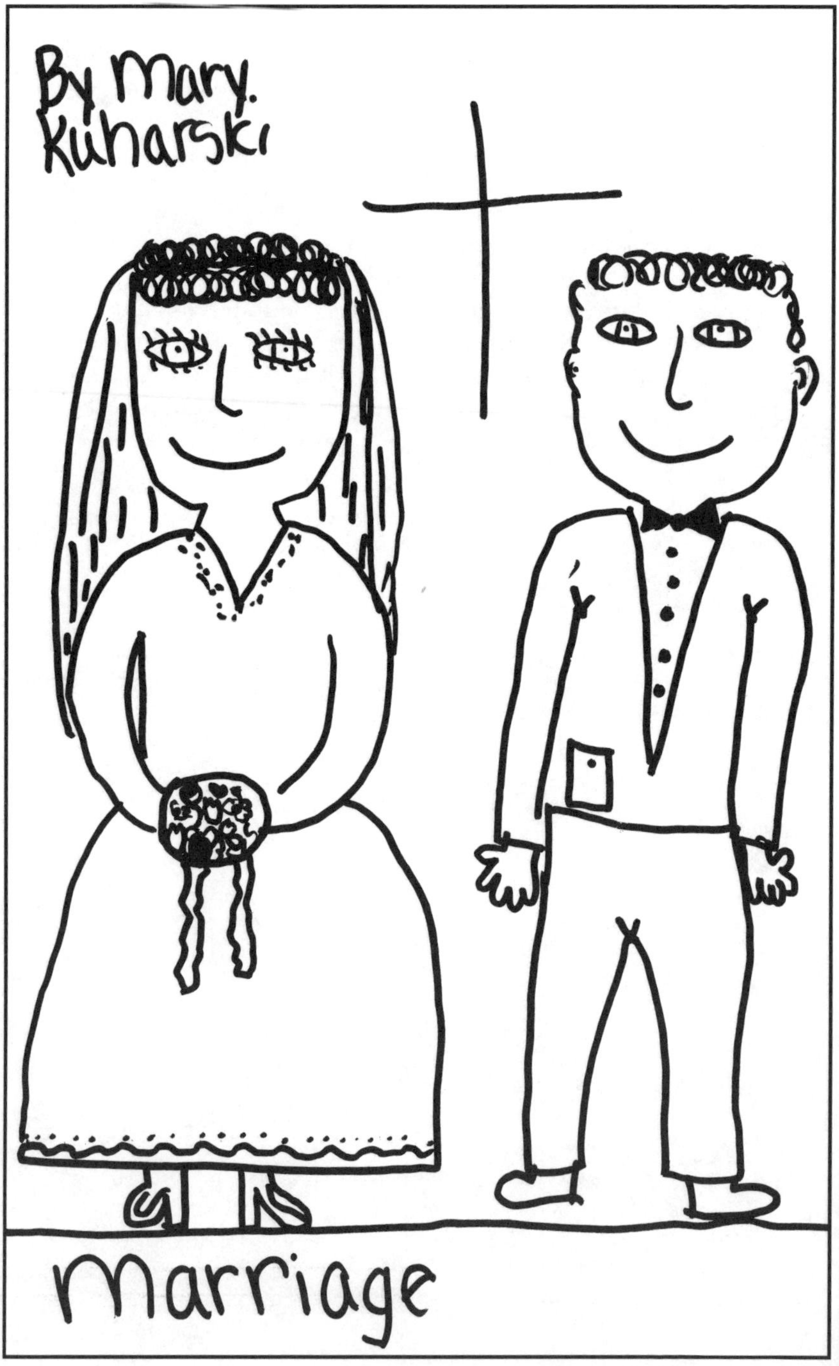
By Mary.
Kuharski
Marriage

14

❦

The Sacraments

I'll never forget the Sunday our family watched a mother in church push her adolescent son down the aisle telling him what to do with the host as they walked up to receive Communion.

Our kids were clearly shocked to hear the woman say to the reluctant boy, "Just take it in your hand and say 'Amen.' Then go back to your seat." When he objected and asked what it meant, she repeated her instruction and said, "I'll tell you later."

Fortunately, the Eucharistic Minister was a religious sister who must have heard enough of the mother-son conversation to ask as they approached her, "How old is your boy?" (He was eleven.) "Has he received his First Holy Communion yet?" When the mother responded negatively but suggested he could do that another time, the sister graciously but firmly refused the sacred host to the child and sent him back to his place.

Sister knew the child had little comprehension of the meaning or significance of the Eucharist, the sacramental presence of the body and blood of Christ. The boy deserved adequate and proper instruction in the faith, and the sacred host deserved protection from disrespect.

Sad to say, in this case both the boy and his mother needed a good basic education on the Eucharist and perhaps the other sacraments as well.

The sacraments — there are seven in all: baptism, confirmation, Holy Eucharist, penance (or reconciliation), anointing of the sick, holy orders, and matrimony — are an outward sign of Christ to give us grace.

The Church teaches that with each sacrament bestowed comes a special "sacramental grace," which helps us carry out the purpose of the sacrament itself. In essence, the sacraments give life to our faith. They are Christ's gift to his

Church, and parents — as the first *missionaries to our children* — have a moral obligation to instill a proper reverence and respect for each one. It is up to us to make sure our young receive both formal and informal education (including setting a good example) in the Catholic faith.

Most parishes now offer adult-education evenings that coincide with the sacraments the children will be receiving. In addition to such faith-enrichment programs, we found that having a catechism on hand is always a good idea.

BAPTISM

A baby's baptism is an exciting event at our house. About the only one who's confused by all the fuss and flurry is the baby! In fact, some of my colicky ones squeaked and squealed their way through the entire ceremony. I tell the kids, "It's the devil's last hurrah! He knows that from here on in, this kid is now part of God's family and will have a special guardian angel watching over him!"

Baptism is the sacrament that makes us members of Christ's Church. It takes away the effects of original sin and any actual sin that may have been committed (if the person being baptized is older). Baptism fills our souls with the new life of sanctifying grace that makes us children of God, members of Christ's Church, and heirs of heaven.

Christ himself told us what to do when he said, "All authority in heaven and on earth has been given to me. Go therefore and make disciples of all nations, baptizing them in the name of the Father and of the Son and of the Holy Spirit" (Matthew 28:18-19).

Catholic parents have an obligation to see to it that their young are baptized as soon as possible. Church law commands parents to have their children baptized within the first weeks after birth. The reason is simply because we recognize baptism as necessary for salvation.

At infant baptism, parents promise *for their child* to renounce the devil and sin and to remain faithful to the gospel teaching and way of life of the Church. We are told in *The Catholic Catechism* that "God promises life everlasting and the means to come to that life; and we freely promise to live in faith, hope, and love." When our children reach maturity, they will have to make their own faith commitment.

Johnny and I were as careful to choose a saint's name for each child as we were in our selection of godparents. We tried to choose couples who we believed were strongly committed to the Church because we felt their presence in our youngster's life would be a spiritual reinforcement to our child and to us. We also felt they would be positive role models in the faith to our young. And what modern-day parent doesn't need reinforcements and role models?

The Code of Canon Law is pretty clear about a godparent's role: He or she should be a Catholic living the faith; mature in years (ordinarily this means over the age of sixteen); and one who is willing and able to fulfill a role of "spiritual concern" for the person being baptized. In other words, a Catholic who is supportive in the faith through prayer and good example.

One of the most fun things we were able to do as our family size grew and the age of our children matured was to select some of our older children to be godparents to the younger ones. Talk about "swelled chests"! Our young adults and teens were thrilled to be that special spiritual person to the new brother or sister in our clan. We figured this gave a whole new (and positive meaning) to the term "peer pressure"!

In the case of naming our children, we believe that their identity with a strong and heavenly hero — a saint — can only work to strengthen their walk in faith as they grow older and understand the meaning of the name and how this person lived for the love of God.

A couple of our adopted children received "conditional baptisms" because they were sickly when they arrived or were older in age. It was possible in their case that they may have initially been baptized before they came to us; but where there is no certainty, the Church permits conditional baptism.

In most instances baptism is performed by a priest or deacon. If there is an emergency, however, anyone may baptize merely by pouring water over the candidate's head and saying, "I baptize you in the name of the Father, and of the Son, and of the Holy Spirit."

"Ya have to get baptized so ya can vote," our young son Charlie once explained to his younger sister Theresa. Hard as we try, some of our efforts at transmitting the faith come more with age and *experience* than with formal instruction.

We celebrate baptisms with great fanfare. We have what we call a "sacrament party," and we surround ourselves with godparents, family, and friends who see this important occasion as one to rejoice in and remember. It's a great beginning for the new baby *and* for us!

Hopefully, these occasions will be wonderful and positive memories for our children — something they in turn will want to pass on to their own young some day.

None of us will ever forget Dominic's baptismal party. We had prepared baked goods, desserts, sliced turkey, and lots of vegetable and fruit dishes for the big day. What we hadn't prepared for that Sunday morning was a snowstorm and blizzard that hit Minneapolis late the night before and prevented most of our guests, including Dominic's godmother and grandparents, from being able to attend.

In spite of the blustery conditions, our family made it to Mass, and the baptism took place with proxies present. As for the party? We invited everyone we talked to at Mass to stop over (we live a block and a half from our parish) for brunch.

The house was full of unexpected and more than welcome guests. Imagine the disappointed children we would have had without a party to kick off Dominic's entrance into the Mystical Body of Christ!

PENANCE

In my view, the sacrament of penance (or reconciliation, as it is more frequently called nowadays) is the sacrament we probably neglect the most. It's also the one we continually need the most. Confession has been denigrated, distorted, and — sad to say in some instances — dismissed altogether.

The sacrament of penance is the *only* sacrament by which any serious sins we've committed are forgiven. Yet today many Catholics pass over their *need* for reconciliation with God. Maybe it's because it's not easy to admit to another when we've done wrong.

Personally speaking, even after all these years and all the practice I've had, I still find it oh so humbling! Yet I know that this is the way Christ calls us closer to him. He could have chosen any way he wanted to forgive sin, but he chose his apostles and their successors (the bishops, and the priests ordained by them) to convey this sacrament. Christ's words were clear: "Receive the Holy Spirit. If you forgive the sins of any, they are forgiven them; if you retain the sins of any, they are retained" (John 20-22-23).

As parents, we want our kids to know that, ultimately, it is not the priest who hears and forgives our sins but Christ himself, who uses the ears, lips, hands, and human body of the priest to transmit his divine forgiveness and grace to us.

"We're so blessed to have the sacrament of reconciliation," I tell my kids. "Just think of how awful it would be to carry the weight of sin on your conscience all the time. It'd be like dragging a dead horse."

Our children need to be encouraged to examine their conscience frequently, to go to confession on a regular basis, and to welcome into their lives the forgiveness and special graces that are offered by Christ through the sacrament of reconciliation.

The priest forgives our sins with these words: "God, the Father of mercies, through the death and resurrection of his Son has reconciled the world to himself and sent the Holy Spirit among us for the forgiveness of sins; through the ministry of the Church may God give you pardon and peace, and I absolve you from your sins in the name of the Father, and of the Son, and of the Holy Spirit" (Rite of Penance).

There's one catch to our being absolved from our previous sins. We must do more than examine our conscience and confess our sins. The catch is a *contrite* heart. We must have true sorrow for our wrongdoing and sincerely intend to avoid that sin in the future.

We also must confess all grave (or, as it was more commonly referred to, "mortal") sin and perform the assigned penance given by the priest.

One of my catechisms says, "Sorrow for sin implies a firm will to avoid all mortal sin in the future. This firm will is called a 'purpose of amendment.' If one has sincerely turned from sin to the Lord, he or she will be determined to remain in grace, and by the strength of His grace, never to turn from Him again. The intention not to sin again does not imply certainty that our weakness will never betray us in the future; but it involves an honest intention to sin gravely no more, and a will to use the means necessary to remain in the state of grace."

Saying an Act of Contrition before the priest is an expression of our sorrow for our sins, even if our motive is not true sorrow because we have offended God but rather because of his "just punishments," that is, "the loss of heaven and the pains of hell."

What's nice to know is that God takes us right where we're at, and even a halfhearted "I'm sorry" is acceptable in God's eyes. He forgives our sins and offers us the grace necessary to say "no" the next time that ugly sin tempts us.

I still approach the confessional with sweaty palms and a healthy fear, yet it never prevents my going because I know well the wonderful feeling of relief and peace of mind that sweeps over me the instant the priest gives me absolution.

It's at times such as these that perhaps I am the most sorry for my non-Catholic brothers and sisters. Let's be honest. Thousands of dollars on psychiatrists and therapists are spent every day by nonbelievers in an effort to relieve guilt and obtain that elusive peace of mind. Catholics, on the other hand, have the counsel of priests, the confidentiality of the confessional, and the healing grace that comes through the sacrament of reconciliation. I'd say that's a peace of mind money can't buy!

I don't think we can remind our children often enough that God loves them. We always want them to know that his love flows constantly no matter what we do. Our sins, however, are obstacles to that flow; and serious (mortal) sin stops it from getting through to our hearts altogether. That's why we need the sacrament of reconciliation.

Normally, the Church requires children (usually about the age of seven years) to receive the sacrament of penance before they receive their First Holy Communion.

In our family, making a first confession has been a very positive and good experience. Our children have come away with warm feelings toward the priests who administered the sacrament, and continue to view their "going to confession" experiences as helpful and beneficial.

I don't rely on my kids to remember to get to confession, however. About every month or so, I *announce* that it's time for *all of us* to go. My method is pretty frank. I simply say: "The telltale signs of sin are leaving their mark around here. I can see some of you are beginning to slide, and before I need to make a list or pack anyone a lunch, we better all get up to church this Saturday and get some fresh grace back into our lives."

This is where our instruction and *example* really count. Our kids need to see that we, too, need God's love and forgiveness.

HOLY EUCHARIST

We loved to play "Mass" when I was a child. We used Mom's long skirts for the bottom, and dish towels or shawls for the top, which became the *respected* habits and vestments we needed to "become sisters and priests."

If we were lucky, we got to use grape juice for the wine. Bread slices with the crusts cut off, flattened and shaped to bite-size wafers, became the hosts. Or, if we were really lucky, we'd have a package of Necco candy wafers and dole them out to the anxious "communicants" one at a time. I liked the chocolate and spicy white ones best!

On occasion, I've seen my own young playing "Body of Christ" with crackers and juice and waferlike candies. It brings back a glimpse of my own youth. More than that, I've come to realize what a wonderful preoccupation such pretending and play (imitating something holy and awe-inspiring) can be for children.

Contrary to the irreverent mother who obviously showed little regard for the true meaning of the Eucharist, we Catholic parents have an obligation to teach our children reverence for the Mass and the Eucharist and to make sure they are adequately prepared before receiving their First Holy Communion.

It goes without saying that adults who skip Mass, who habitually come late and leave early (without good reason), or who demonstrate an apathy or irreverence toward the Eucharist or priest cause serious scandal to their children who follow more by imitation than instruction.

The Eucharist is a sacrament and, like all sacraments, it is a sign of Christ. But unlike the other sacraments, the Eucharist is not only an action of Christ but also *really contains* Christ himself, under the appearances of bread and wine.

Catholics believe that Christ first gave himself to the Church in this way at the Last Supper before he died. It was then that Christ said, "This is my body" as he held up the bread, and "This is my blood" as he held up the wine, changing the substances into his body and blood and instructing his apostles, "Do this in remembrance of me" (see Luke 22:19-20).

Christ continues to perform this miracle (called transubstantiation) at the Sacrifice of the Mass *every day* through his priests. Each time we receive the Eucharist then, we are not only receiving the *real presence* of Jesus Christ but also actively commemorating and participating in the Sacrifice on the Cross. This participation at Mass is the highest form of prayer.

The word "Eucharist" means thanksgiving, and our Lord in a most special way gave thanks to the Father as he offered it. It is more than a common meal meant for sharing; we must remind our young that it is a sacred banquet and that we are privileged to participate.

Frequently, Catholics today run into situations, especially during weddings, special holidays, or funerals, when individuals who are not practicing Catholics may express a desire to receive Holy Communion "like everyone else." Or, a worse scenario, a family member who has strayed from the faith suggests it's "all right" to receive, with no intention of returning to the Church.

Although some of these issues should generally be referred to a priest or other competent authority, it is a spiritual work of mercy — if the opportunity presents itself — to instruct such individuals on the meaning of the Eucharist and Church teaching regarding the reception of Holy Communion. If at all possible, they should be asked to refrain from receiving Communion. To do less would, by our own acquiescence, trivialize the significance of the sacred host.

The Catholic Catechism reminds us that the following conditions must be met in order to receive Holy Communion worthily:

● One must be a baptized Catholic (except for specific situations outlined in Church law).

● One must believe what the Church teaches about this sacrament.

● One must be in the state of grace. If a mortal sin has been committed, a sacramental confession must first be made before Holy Communion can be received again.

● One must have the right intention, that is, to love God, to grow in grace and unity with Christ's Mystical Body.

● One must abstain from food and drink (except for water and medication) as Church law requires.

Reception of the Blessed Sacrament does more than renew us with sanctifying grace. It gives us more vigorous protection from committing serious sin. And, most importantly, the Eucharist in a very real sense *draws us* to Christ and *brings us closer* to the Blessed Trinity.

Next to our children's baptism, the reception of their First Holy Communion is the single most important event in their young lives. The Eucharist is the core of our faith. With that in mind, our family marks this spiritual milestone with a special celebration. We want our children to know this is a significant day to remember and one worth special preparation.

Some tips we've found to make this sacrament and others memorable and special to our children include:

✔ **Get a special outfit.** For the rest of the family, it doesn't have to be new or terribly fancy, just clean, pressed, and looking like your "Sunday best." For the communicant, we feel the selection of a special "First Communion" outfit (white shirt and tie for the boy; white dress and veil for the girl) is important. It's a day the communicant will always remember, particularly the significance of wearing white for the purity of his or her heart; moreover, the newness of the outfit reminds the child of the special attention this sacrament deserves.

✔ **Make it fun and memorable.** For baptisms and First Communions we have a party. The kids refer to these occasions as our "sacrament parties," and we try to make them fun times to remember. For confirmation we take the family to an inexpensive restaurant for dinner. Especially for a big family on a tight budget, this also makes the event special.

✔ **Take plenty of pictures.** Home movies (and snapshots to be placed in a child's baby book or scrapbook) are just the kind of memorabilia that help recall the importance and joy of such a happy occasion.

✔ **Purchase or make a special gift.** Again, it doesn't have to be expensive or elaborate — just special. Something with a spiritual emphasis is best — a crucifix on a necklace, a prayer book appropriate for the child's age, a book on the lives of the saints, a book about his or her namesake, a rosary, small statue, or plaque for the child's room. Encourage your children, even the younger ones, to give a gift. A small homemade card or gift from every child helps those little ones feel an active part of the celebration and helps them mark the event in their own minds.

✔ **Splurge a little.** Whether this sacramental celebration is an inexpensive dinner out or a party at home, make it one to remember. We have plenty of home-baked treats and a smorgasbord dinner shared with lots of family and friends. Remember, while a little wine for adults may be appropriate, heavy drinking will likely destroy the sanctity and wonderful memories the day was meant to hold for the communicant and those celebrating with him or her.

✔ **Pitch in.** If at all possible, let all of your family members help with the preparations. This means yard work, house-cleaning, table-setting, shoe-shining, and clothes selection, as well as serving guests, hostessing, and, of course, the after-party cleanup. Children love to belong and feel an active part of an event. When they are included in the preparation of a sacrament party, they have a higher stake in assuring its success.

✔ **Spiritual preparation is a must.** In all of our busyness, we must not forget to make sure that *we and our children* have been to confession recently and are spiritually prepared to receive Communion at the baptism, First Communion, confirmation, wedding, or ordination that we are attending.

CONFIRMATION

The year our Mary Elizabeth, then a thirteen-year-old eighth grader, prepared to receive her confirmation, she and her classmates began months in advance to study the sacrament in depth to prepare for its reception. As part of this preparation the students were asked to complete a "service project" that required them to perform several hours of work or community service.

"Yippee, skippy!" I told her. "I've got just the projects in mind. These kitchen cupboards all need cleaning; the hallway walls with Dominic's and Joe's designs are begging to be washed; and the basement workroom and play area are such a mess they look like the result of last summer's twister! When do you start?"

Grinning, Mary replied, "Nice try, Mom. But no dice. Doing stuff around here doesn't count. Father said that volunteer work is important because it will help us see that there are *others* who need our help. He said there are many ways we can serve God by serving others." (Oh, really? Tell me about it!)

The girls were encouraged to do baby-sitting, grocery shopping for shut-ins, or volunteer work in nursing homes or hospitals. The young boys in the class chose house-painting, yard work (raking, mowing, cleaning), or hospital work.

"We aren't suppose to do this just once — for confirmation and then quit — but throughout our lives," Mary reported. "It's part of our Christian commitment and witness, Father said." (Don't ya love it?)

Mary's "service project" was to work one day a week during summer vacation as a candy striper at St. Mary's Hospital in Minneapolis. When school began, she and a classmate found a volunteer job at a local nursing home serving trays of food or spoon-feeding the sick and elderly residents.

Actually, I was delighted to see this "newest teen" of ours donating her services and, of course, I still couldn't resist suggesting that she'd probably chalk up even more graces if she'd empty the overflowing trash basket in the kitchen, or vacuum an extra room around home once in a while! Just keeping her own room free of debris is a corporal work of mercy! (Once a mother — always a mother!)

The catechism reminds us to be patient: "The special presence of the Spirit made real in us by confirmation is a constant call to growth in Christian life. Confirmation does not bring one to maturity at once. But it is a pressing divine call toward, and a promise of divine assistance in, living our Christian vocation maturely." I guess parents can't expect miracles *overnight.*

I don't think many of my kids (if any) fully understood the significance of the sacrament of confirmation when they were confirmed. But then neither did I. I tell them, "It is a mystery of our faith that goes to work on us, to nourish us, strengthen us, protect us from evil, and bring us closer to Christ, even when we can't fully comprehend how it works."

In baptism we are born again of water and the Holy Spirit. In confirmation the Holy Spirit gives us power and strength to grow in the life of grace. Moreover, the Holy Spirit comes to us in a special way through the anointing of holy chrism (a mixture of oil and balm) by the bishop. The anointing is in the form of a cross because the strength given is strength to bear crosses for the love of God.

Being a strong witness, or "soldier of Christ," in today's secular society is no easy task. Confirmation offers that spiritual boost when we need it. When I think of confirmation, I remember Christ's promise before he ascended into heaven, "I am with you always, to the end of the age" (Matthew 28:20). Truly, this sacrament helps us to become like a "soldier of Christ," enabling us to fight against evil — namely the world, the flesh, and the devil.

Like the other sacraments, confirmation increases sanctifying grace, offers its own sacramental grace, and imprints an indelible and lasting character on the soul.

This is the sacrament that helps us most to live our Christian life loyally and to be witnesses to our faith and love for the Church. We join ourselves to Christ, and take on his armor every time we use the spiritual weapons we receive through confirmation:

✔ **Sufferings and sacrifices.** When offered for the love of God, these tools enrich our soul and the souls of those we pray for.

✔ **Prayer.** We can literally pray people into heaven by offering our Mass intentions, prayers, and daily sacrifices for deceased loved ones and friends.

✔ **Good example**. We must never forget that it is *our* faith and Christian witness that may bring a non-Catholic to the Church.

✔ **Encouragement.** *All* Catholics are to be *missionaries*, encouraging others — be they our children, other family members, neighbors, or friends — to know and love the Church.

One man told a story about always being invited by his neighbor to play golf. "There were so many Saturdays Bill asked me to play golf with him. But not once did he invite me to go to church with him. I knew which was more important to Bill. Obviously, golf."

Are we too proud (or — God forbid! — too embarrassed) to invite a neighbor or friend to Mass or to consider taking an inquiry class in the Catholic faith? So what's the worse thing that can happen to us if we ask?

ANOINTING OF THE SICK

I think there was more mystery connected with this sacrament years ago. Before Vatican II, it was more commonly referred to as Extreme Unction and was used primarily when an individual was gravely ill or close to death.

Today the sacrament of the anointing of the sick is still used in those circumstances but is also used for the elderly or to reach those who are suffering from serious mental and/or physical (though not life-threatening) conditions.

My dear friend Mary suffers from Crohn's disease, an affliction with no known cure. I was privileged to be present when she received the sacrament of the anointing of the sick one Saturday morning.

It was a beautiful service bestowed by our parish priests on Mary and others in our community, many of whom I knew, yet had no idea until then that they, too, were struggling with serious pain or illness.

As I knelt and prayed for Mary, I looked around at the rows of pews filled with individuals waiting to receive this healing sacrament, or were there in support of someone who was. Perhaps there would be no obvious "cures" that resulted from the ministering hands of the priests, I thought. There would be, however, a source of grace from the sacrament itself, and a consolation and comfort in knowing that this whole body of believers — Christ's Mystical Body — would be lifting them up in prayer. A pretty powerful gift for an early Saturday morning, don't you agree? Mary told me later how touched and very blessed she felt by the service. Me, too! (Which brings to mind: What do atheists and agnostics do for pain? Sometimes Tylenol just doesn't cut it.)

Father Mark Dosh, a pastor of a large suburban Minnesota parish and a former professor of philosophy and theology at St. Paul Seminary, says, "The sacrament of the anointing of the sick is a way of joining us *and our suffering* more deeply with the suffering of Christ. It makes certain that this suffering becomes part of the treasury of the saints."

The anointing of the sick is a sacrament through which the blessed oil by the priest and his prayer give health and strength to the soul and sometimes to the body. This sacrament, like all the others, offers special grace, comforts those in sickness, and gives the recipient the strength needed to fight temptation. Moreover, it is offered as a preparation for our entrance into heaven by the remission of our sins and a cleansing of our souls from the remains of sin.

In my view, God thought of everything! Including how to head off the devil at the pass. After all, this beautiful sacrament comes at a time when we might be the most weak in our struggle to fight off temptations of despair and hopelessness.

Make no mistake. Accidents, grave illness, or life-threatening circumstances are the devil's "last-ditch run" to get us into his "camp." He's got to work fast and feverishly before it's too late and we are, for all eternity, enjoying the fullness of God in heaven.

One of the things I learned from reading the lives of some of the great saints was that many told of great mental and spiritual tortures they suffered during their illness or final hours of life on earth. Yuk! The devil just never gives up till he *knows* the battle is over.

Our best weapon is prayer. The late Bishop Fulton Sheen used to say, "Don't let all that suffering go to waste. Offer it up."

Aren't we blessed to have this sacrament, the prayers of our friends on earth, *and the saints* to pray for us and strengthen us? Even the Hail Mary urges the Blessed Mother to plead our case "now and at the hour of our death."

Unlike most other faiths, the Catholic Church views suffering and sickness as opportunities for grace and holiness. This is noteworthy because some actually see illness and injury as a punishment or "lesson needed to be learned."

St. Peter reminds us, however, to "rejoice, insofar as you are sharing Christ's sufferings so that you may also be glad and shout for joy when his glory is revealed" (1 Peter 4:13). In essence we are "co-redeemers with Christ," and this sacrament enables us to participate fully with the grace and strength Christ offers to us.

I truly believe that while the sacrament of the anointing of the sick gives grace and spiritual strength to the sick person, it is also a source of support and peace of mind to the sick person's family and loved ones who often must stand on the sidelines feeling helpless and anxious. The anointing of the sick is a visible sign of God's promise and his love. It is also a witness to the faith.

I remember the time I took the children to the hospital to visit an elderly friend who had just received the "last sacraments," as it is sometimes called (along with penance and Viaticum, or Holy Communion, for those in danger of death), and was obviously near death.

The kids' faces grew sober, and their eyes registered helplessness as they stared at the man who lay "wired" with tubes, yet lifeless to their chatter.

We fumbled with small talk and reminiscing for a few minutes until I suggested we would close our visit after reciting a few decades of the Rosary. As we stood around the old man's bed, his roommate and attending nurses looked on in silence. I thought little more about it until the man's son called a few days later and said, "Dad's roommate was quite moved by your family's visit and the fact that you cared enough to pray in front of everyone. He said he had *never* seen anyone do that so publicly before."

The sacrament of the anointing of the sick is administered by a deacon, priest, bishop, or pope; but we lay people are also called, as members of the common union (communion) of saints, to pray for the sick in our midst.

HOLY ORDERS

I remember when our Charlie was very young. He asked in all seriousness after Mass one day, "Don't priests ever get hungry or tired, Mom?" When I answered, "Of course, they do," he asked, "Well, how do they ever get to eat or sleep if they have to be in church all day?"

Poor Charlie was just sure that the priests spent twenty-four hours of every day either saying Mass, hearing confession, or waiting patiently in the sacristy for the next service to begin. He had never seen a priest outside his churchly setting, so his concept of what a priestly vocation meant was pretty limited!

Once we began to invite priests to dinner, our children saw them in a social atmosphere, visiting, laughing, playing basketball in the backyard, going for walks, and playing cards and board games with the family. The mystery and fear were removed.

Our kids aren't the only ones with misconceptions, as the following comment brings out: "He looks so old on the altar, but does he play a tough game of basketball!" one eighth-grade boy was heard to remark about Father Mark Dosh, after an exciting and close basketball game between the faculty and eighth graders.

"Priests are ordinary human beings attempting to live extraordinary lives for the love of Christ," we've frequently told our young. This is something all are called by God to do but particularly priests in a very special way.

Holy orders is the only sacrament that is exclusively for men. It is the sacrament through which men receive the power and grace to perform the sacred duties of bishop, priest, or deacon.

While the Church sees the call to religious orders, such as the various congregations of brothers and sisters, as a worthy vocation, holy orders is reserved for those men called to become priests or deacons.

Before their ordination by a bishop, candidates to the priesthood must have spent a sufficient time in preparation and study. They must be persons of good character, lead virtuous lives, and have the ability to perform the duties of the priestly life.

"The sacraments of holy orders and matrimony are closely connected," my pastor, Father Frank Kittock, has often said. "In fact, holy orders depends upon good sacramental marriages in order to nurture and support God's call to the priesthood and religious life."

It really is up to us as parents to see to it that our children have an openness to the possibility of a priestly vocation. That openness to God's call and the ability to respond with love and acceptance, however, can be damaged or destroyed if a child grows up in an atmosphere that belittles or downplays the married state or that of a priestly vocation.

How do we speak and act toward the priests and religious who serve us? Do we attempt to expose our children in a more personal way to priests and sisters? Even if we disagree with a priest or church leader, do our children understand and see our obedience to the Church and her teachings? Do we encourage our children to be open to a priestly call by God or to consider a religious vocation as a sister or brother?

MATRIMONY

A little boy was added to our neighborhood community not too long ago. His father, who rents the house across the street from ours, walked him over and initiated the introductions. He'd heard tell of the "house with thirteen kids" and had hopes his son would find one among our ranks with matching age and interests. Not a difficult task to accomplish. Indeed, we did have a child or two (or three or four) who could identify and recreate with this curious and eager third grader. Yet age and interests may be the only similarities this young lad shares with our siblings.

Mark (not his real name) is the product of divorce and so, as is common in such split arrangements, he "lives" with ("visits" is a far more honest term) his dad one or two weekends a month. The rest of his life revolves around his mom, school, day care, and latchkey arrangement.

He's a personable chap who has little fear of new people or places, and since that first meeting he's been over on those infrequent occasions sharing episodes of roller-skating, backyard football toss, kick-the-can games, or what have you, with my children.

The other night, as I sat outside with my after-dinner cup of coffee watching the backyard play, Mark was there. When he spotted me, he left our pack at play talking excitedly as he approached me. "Guess what?" he started. "My dad's getting married in a couple of months and I get to go to the wedding. I've never been to a wedding before and I'm really excited to see one."

"Sounds exciting. Whom is he going to marry?" I asked.

"Her name's Anne."

"Have you been doing some fun things with them on weekends?" I asked, realizing I hadn't seen him around for a couple of months.

"No, I just met her two days ago," he responded.

By this time most of our brood had gathered around our outdoor table and were listening attentively to the lad as he vividly detailed his impression of the upcoming event.

"We all know about weddings, too," I told Mark, "because we had one in our family just last August when these guys' big sister got married." Instantly, the Kuharski kids all smiled spontaneously, nodding their heads in agreement as they seemed to immediately recall the gala ceremony and the fun and fuss that surrounded such a happy occasion.

As Mark continued to ramble on about his father's future wedding, my children (then ages three to thirteen) stood around, at first trying to share in his excitement and anticipation. The more Mark talked, however, the more confused and puzzled my kids' faces grew as they attempted to envision and understand the scenario.

"Anne isn't from this area, so we'll be going to her town for the wedding," he said. "I've never been there before, so that will be fun, too. Plus, I get to wear something new and that's not a bad deal either," he added.

"And you know what else?" he offered. "There's a great sporting-goods store there and I can buy my hockey skates and equipment for this fall and winter the same time I'm there for the wedding. I'm sure my mom will be coming to the wedding so she can bring me to the store to get all the stuff I need," he went on resolutely.

His mom attend his dad's wedding? Mark must have caught my disbelief at the thought, but before I could utter a sound, he reassuringly insisted, "I'm sure my mom will be coming to Dad's wedding. She'll come. It'll be great — and a perfect time to get my hockey stuff."

By now the full impact of what was being discussed was beginning to sink in, and there was a happiness-turned-horror on my kids' faces as they attempted to draw the mental picture of themselves in the same scene — attending their dad's wedding to another woman with me at their side. The conversation with Mark came to a polite end. No one dared challenge his perception or assumptions. "There's no way his mother's going to be attending that wedding," I thought to myself as I walked back toward the kitchen door. But, then again, in this civilized culture of "friendly divorce" maybe Mark is right and I am the misguided soul.

Mark is but one lone statistic in today's era of no-fault divorce. The child who is left in the wake. What will his lifetime experiences teach him about marriage, the meaning of "forever," commitment, and real love? Who will he one day marry? And what are his chances of knowing the difference between marriage and a sacrament? I don't know. But Mark and the many like him are worth praying for.

* * *

"Husbands, love your wives, just as Christ loved the church and gave himself up for her" (Ephesians 5:25).

The Church teaches that matrimony is the sacrament by which baptized men and women *bind themselves for life* in a lawful marriage. A valid and binding marriage exists when:

● Both partners are baptized. If one partner is not baptized, the marriage is still binding and valid but is not a sacrament.

- The marriage occurs before a priest (or bishop) and two witnesses (or is dispensed from this).

- Both partners give free and full consent to the marriage.

- Both partners intend a bond of faithful love *and* are open to the possibility of children.

Catholics see marriage, not as a partnership of two, but of three — with God as the Third Partner. In sacramental marriage, God promises to provide the grace and means necessary to help the couple to be faithful to each other and to provide for the welfare of any children they may have.

Unlike all the other sacraments that are administered by a bishop, priest, or deacon, matrimony is the only one bestowed by the candidates themselves. The husband and wife confer the sacrament on each other. (In emergency baptisms, lay people are extraordinary ministers of the sacrament. In matrimony, lay people are the ordinary ministers of the sacrament.)

One of the most wonderful and fun things experienced by our family was the wedding of our oldest daughter, Chrissy, to Andy Klaesges. What a blessing! Both raised Catholic, they centered their wedding preparations on making this sacrament holy and one to be remembered. And it was.

I do admit to some secular goals as well: Chrissy's goal was making sure *all* her brothers and sisters had a part in either the ceremony or celebration. No easy task! John's goal was working to make sure he could pay for it. And my goal was to make sure no one went down the aisle bare naked!

We succeeded on all fronts — except for a near miss when Joseph (then two) rolled in the church garden an hour *before the wedding* and had to be taken home and completely "laundered."

Challenges aside, Chrissy and Andy and their obvious love for each other, their family, and faith were just about the best role models and examples we could have asked for. All of the other Kuharskis witnessed firsthand the goodness and romance of dating, the preparation time of an engagement, and the excitement and sacredness of a Catholic wedding. I pray for the same kind of married union for our other children.

When we offer ourselves to each other in a sacramental

union, we are promising to be faithful to God and to each other until death. God, in return, promises to those marrying — just as he makes the *same promise* to the one being ordained — that he will let flow all the grace necessary to sustain us in our vocation. Thus, a couple who do not take matrimony seriously; those who separate without grave reason or separate with the intent to remarry; or the priest who walks away from his vocation without dispensation — all are committing sin and causing scandal to Christ's Church. So also do those who marry outside the Church (thereby disregarding their Catholic faith) ignore the grace and covenant offered in this sacrament.

The Church tells us that matrimony is more than a commitment or a promise. It is a covenant between God and the couple, and that is why it is so sacred and cannot be broken.

Of course, there are times in even the best of marriages when togetherness, unity, and love seem all but "dead." Still, as Catholics we trust God's promise and continue in our married commitment, relying on the grace and the means that he promises will be there. Jesus told us that "what God has joined together, let no one separate" (Mark 10:9).

The Church teaches that the "chief duties of husband and wife are to be faithful to each other, and to provide in every way for the welfare of the children God may give them." The *St. Joseph Baltimore Catechism* goes on to suggest that "married people must learn to love unselfishly, to forget themselves so that they can spend themselves for each other."

Now there's a lesson that will come *naturally* once kids enter the picture! Children have a unique way of *stretching* what we thought were limits to our unselfishness and love.

A couple's commitment to live in a union of marital love "is a sign and a participation in the love that Christ has for his Church." It is a "sign that confers the grace it signifies." In other words, while the world declares that one out of three marriages ends in divorce, we remain faithful. God's grace can transform even weak human love to one that is enduring, faithful, and fruitful.

"Children are the supreme gift of marriage," we are clearly and beautifully reminded by the Second Vatican Council document *Pastoral Constitution on the Church in the Modern World*. They are not only the visible fruits of a couple's love but a proof of a profound sharing as the husband and wife literally become co-creators with the love of God.

Artificial contraception is forbidden, then, because it separates the marital act from its procreative dimension, attempting to block God's creative power. The spouse is viewed not as God's potential co-creator working with nature but merely as one to give sexual pleasure and satisfaction. The generosity, the openness, and the unselfishness that God calls us to have been abandoned for self.

In his encyclical *Humanae Vitae*, Pope Paul VI describes the four qualities of married love: (1) human, (2) total, (3) permanent, and (4) fruitful.

It was this encyclical that reaffirmed for modern times the Church's teaching against artificial contraception. Couples were encouraged to be faithful, prayerful, thoughtful, open, and *generous* to God's gift of new life. While natural family planning is encouraged as responsible parenting, it is *not* to be used to defer being open to a child unless the spouses believe there is a grave reason. That's where I always got hung up. I could think of a lot of little reasons, but I never could, for very long, come up with one "grave" enough!

Perhaps one of the greatest tasks we parents have is to *demonstrate* to our young our respect for the sacrament of matrimony — both in our own lives and in the lives of those we know.

To encourage a good and right attitude toward marriage, we parents might ask ourselves: Do our children know that we see our marriage as a sacred union? Do we confuse our children by attending outside-the-Church second or third marriages? Do we ever ask them to pray for us? If they hear or see us quarrel, do they likewise see affection and love? Do they see us pray together? Do we let them know we view them and *all* human life, born and preborn, as sacred?

15

❦

Sacramentals and Sanctifying Grace

My agnostic friend Jean called one day and said, "You Catholics seem to have a prayer and a blessing for just about everything. Can you say something before I go in for this surgery? I'd really feel much better about it."

Jean's lack of faith, yet obvious respect for mine, is a puzzle. It's hard for me to understand someone who believes there is a benefit to prayer, yet can't make the plunge herself.

I did pray with Jean and couldn't resist adding, "Now try it yourself, Sweetheart! It's so easy to talk to God. He'll be so glad to hear from you, he won't care how the words come out."

All in all, she's right about one thing: We Catholics do have a blessing for just about every occasion. In addition to special prayers, it's not unusual to see crucifixes, statues, and pictures of our Lord, the Blessed Mother, and the saints in our churches, schools, and our homes.

All of these things — the blessings as well as blessed objects, such as holy water, candles, ashes, palms, crucifixes, medals, rosaries, scapulars, and images of Christ and the saints — are called sacramentals.

As a cradle Catholic, I used to take the presence of sacramentals in the home, in one form or another, pretty much for granted. Then I met Sue, a young mother of three who was a member of our prayer group. Her husband would *not allow* her to display a holy picture or crucifix in their home. He also was not happy about her increased devotion to the faith. Why?

"When we met, I was at the height of my rebellion," Sue explained one day. "I hadn't been attending Mass on a regular basis and was defining my own standard of faith. Because my husband was a man of no previous religious beliefs, there was no problem."

Sue went on to say that after they got married, she started a slow return to the Church. And when she began to have children she wanted them to have the same environment that she had grown up in — a Catholic home. Her husband, however, did not understand her spiritual about-face.

Instead of arguing, Sue used a far more powerful weapon: prayer and patience. She attended Sunday Mass with her children and participated in church events and a prayer group. But she made sure these activities did not conflict with other family activities. She quietly lived her faith.

Her husband's attitude began to change, not overnight, but gradually. He'd attend church with her and the children at Christmas and Easter or a special service that involved the children. Eventually, a crucifix came to be displayed in their home, followed later by a few holy pictures on the children's bedroom walls. Moreover, the children attended CCD classes, and Sue herself taught a preschool CCD class.

The last time I saw Sue, she was offering a prayer of thanksgiving for her husband's changed heart. "Jack decided this year it would be worth the financial sacrifice to put the kids in our local Catholic grade school," she said. And the bonus? Jack had begun attending Mass weekly with Sue and the children. He liked the changes he was experiencing.

We might not hear a lot about sacramentals, but they are used frequently by the Church. And we, too, are encouraged to use them within our homes and families.

The church defines sacramentals as "visible signs given by the Church to remind us of God, the saints, and the spiritual truths of our faith."

Sacramentals inspire our prayer, devotion to God, and acts of love and service to others. When this happens, we receive sanctifying grace and a renewed resolution to resist evil.

Using sacramentals with faith, the catechism tells us, "means believing in what they represent and treating them as signs of spiritual things. We break the First Commandment by superstition, however, if we were ever to use them as good luck charms."

The most familiar sacramentals at our house are holy pictures, the crucifix, the rosary, holy water, scapular, and Lenten palms on the wall.

We have a crucifix or holy picture in every room. The way I see it, with fifteen people under one roof, Satan may be lurking around just about any corner. It's much harder to think about sinning, or hanging on the phone and plotting evil, I figure, if a crucifix — or a picture of the Blessed Mother or that of St. Michael the Archangel — is staring back at you. I'll use anything!

HOLY WATER

We use holy water around our house to accent the importance of just about any event — buying a new car, moving to a new home, or preparing a special meal at Easter time. I also make use of it for those stubborn or serious illnesses that can so often lay low an entire family.

The night before Johnny's scheduled brain surgery, our family knelt down and said the Rosary. Then each of us took holy water and made the Sign of the Cross on Johnny's forehead where the tumor was located. I must admit it was a funny sight to see his poor face dripping with holy water as each kid insisted on getting a turn to add one more blessing. But there's nothing like a little laughter — especially at a time like this!

Was the holy water responsible for the successful surgery? Only our heavenly Father knows. All we know is that the prayers and holy water were a source of strength to us.

It's become an annual ritual on the first day of the school year to bless our children with holy water by making the Sign of the Cross on each of their foreheads. Some of our teens were initially embarrassed, but they never refused. (Hmmm. . .) I even bless the neighbor kids who call for my kids on their way to school. I'm convinced they all enjoy the attention.

One time, while I was ushering the high schoolers out the door, my Michael, then three, crawled up on the counter and drank the whole bottle of holy water that was sitting there. That night I told the kids at the dinner table, "Maybe this is a sign Michael is going to be a priest! Who knows, maybe a bishop or cardinal!" A sense of humor is always helpful in parenting.

SCAPULAR

The devotion and use of the scapular — a custom once practiced by most Catholics — has fallen off, sad to say, like so many beautiful earlier devotions. (There are various kinds of scapulars, among them the brown scapular of the Carmelite Order, the white scapular of the Sacred Hearts of Jesus and Mary, and the blue scapular of the Immaculate Conception.) Since I became a Third Order Carmelite, I have worn a scapular daily. Most of my children, however, are still not accustomed to wearing a scapular, and because I believe some of these things come with prayer and time, I never insist.

A scapular consists of two small squares of cloth joined by strings so that they can be worn over the shoulder — one in the back and one in the front. The wearing of the scapular is a requirement of the Third Orders. I see it as an outward sign that we belong to God. What's more, I feel as if there is a spiritual shield of protection over me, a mantle of love.

CANDLES

I'm not much into candles. I'm always afraid something or someone will catch fire. But at baptisms, First Holy Communions, confirmations, and holidays, we bring out a blessed candle or one of the kids' baptismal candles and use it as a centerpiece. It adds a note of reverence to the occasion.

SANCTIFYING GRACE

It must be hard for little kids to envision sanctifying grace. (Often it's even hard for us adults!)

You may recall the story in Chapter 9 of how Dominic at age four would mispronounce "grace" as "glaze" when saying the Hail Mary. Well, when our Tina learned the Hail Mary, it sounded as if the Blessed Mother was a bowl of fruit because she would say, "Hail Mary, full of *grapes*."

To Tina, being "full of grapes" probably sounded a lot more plausible than being "full of grace." Indeed, I'm not sure parents can ever fully explain the meaning of grace to children. I usually fall back on the example of Popeye, the cartoon sailor, who relies on a can of spinach to reinforce his muscle and energy.

"Grace is like spiritual spinach," I tell my kids. "It gives us invisible power to fight off evil and keep us close to God." (It might not be exactly theological, but they get the idea.)

The catechism says that "sanctifying grace is divine life in our soul. By it Christ lives in us and we in Him."

The Church teaches that grace makes us holy, makes us adopted children of God (a notion not unfamiliar at our house), makes us "temples of the Holy Spirit," and gives us the right to heaven. Of course, this grace is damaged by sin and can be lost altogether if we intentionally commit serious (mortal) sin, which cuts us off from God's love.

I remind my kids — and I need to be reminded, too — that "God is all-merciful and forgiving. God *is* love, and that love flows to us constantly no matter what we do. It is only our sinful acts that put up a wall, blocking God's love and will for our life." Going to confession frequently, whether we *think* we need it or not, keeps God's love flowing and the wall down.

My kids aren't going to remember it all, but it is good for us big kids to know what we are told about grace: "It radically changes us and makes us sharers in God's nature and life. God gives the just person the virtues of faith, hope, and love, so that we may be able to do the works of God." These virtues are called the "theological virtues" because they orient our new life directly toward God.

There are other virtues as well, such as the cardinal virtues of prudence, justice, temperance, and fortitude. Moreover, the Church has persistently taught that the gifts of wisdom, understanding, counsel, knowledge, fortitude, piety, and fear of the Lord are conferred on all the faithful with the gift of sanctifying grace.

Our pastor says that these gifts "are given by God to work in direct opposition to what we call the seven capital sins," which are pride, covetousness, lust, anger, gluttony, envy, and sloth. Isn't that comforting to know? A virtue for every vice!

I can't follow my kids around with a catechism, and they

sure aren't going to sit still if I start preaching; but when an opportunity arises, I remind them about the faith we live.

Not long ago Angie and Kari (then ten and nine respectively) passed up a chance to go swimming with a friend in order to go with my godchild Catherine and her mom to visit the retired nuns at a local convent. They sang and tap-danced to the elderly sisters' great delight!

Afterward, I reminded the girls that this was very pleasing to God — a corporal work of mercy — and that they would get a special grace because of it. I'm sure they didn't fully comprehend, but all three smiled with pride, perhaps because they sensed our approval and pleasure. "Let's go have a treat" is the way Catherine's mom and I sometimes mark such occasions.

We remind our children that we obtain grace every time we go to Mass, receive the Eucharist, go to confession, or receive any of the other sacraments. We also get grace when we pray and perform even the most insignificant of deeds if we offer them as prayers to God. These little prayers, like sacramentals, give us grace and keep us close to God.

My mom ingrained in me the phrase "All for thee, O Sacred Heart of Jesus." It stuck and it worked. Now I'd like my own to know that grace is just one simple phrase away. All they need to do — whether they're cleaning their room, doing their homework, or bearing a hurt or illness — is to "offer it up."

"Ya mean even practicing the piano?" Mary Elizabeth asked one day.

"Yup," I replied. "Even piano practice."

16

❦

Making a Good Confession

The sacrament of penance (or reconciliation) is perhaps one of the most important yet overlooked sacraments. There may be no real way we can visualize the grace and power that come to us each time we go to confession and receive absolution for our sins, but I tell my kids to imagine in their minds that grace works in our lives the way spinach does for Popeye, the cartoon character.

"After being chased and caught by Bluto, imagine poor Popeye tied to the railroad tracks and left to die. Just as the train is approaching, whistle blowing and clattering down the tracks toward Popeye, along comes Olive Oil with a full bag of groceries. Out of her bag falls a can of spinach, which plops right into Popeye's hand. He tears open the can with his teeth, gulps the contents down, and instantly he's transformed with power and might. He breaks the ropes binding him and rolls off the tracks — just in the nick of time, of course — and gives Bluto such a tremendous left hook that Bluto sees a swarm of birdies chirping overhead."

So, too, in a very real and supernatural way, I tell my kids, "The grace we get from the sacrament of reconciliation gives us all the power and might we need to resist *any* temptation that comes our way." After all, God wants us to be happy. He does not want us to be tied down by sin.

Unfortunately, society today has lost its sense of sin. While there is much talk about l-o-v-e, there is little said about fault, wrongdoing, guilt, shame, or sin.

We must always remind our children of the love and mercy of God. His forgiveness, no matter our wrongdoing, is ever present and knows no bounds. Nevertheless, the seriousness of sin must never be diminished. To diminish sin would diminish the cross and the very reason Christ suffered and died for us. In fact, he went to the cross as if you or I were the only one in the world in need of his redemptive love.

The Church teaches that there are two kinds of sin that weaken our souls and attempt to sever our relationship with God.

● *Venial sin*, though considered a less serious offense against God's law, seems to set in motion a chain of events to draw us away from God and toward evil. Just as one lie seems to set off a string of other coverup lies, so also do acts of gossip, selfishness, greed, etc., weaken our character and tempt us to other acts of wrongdoing. Venial sin harms us by making us less fervent in our love and service to God as well as weakening our power to resist mortal sin.

● *Mortal sin* is a grievous, or serious, offense against the law of God. This sin, called mortal, is considered deadly because it deprives us of our spiritual food — sanctifying grace — and cuts us off from God's love. When we commit mortal sin, we literally make our soul an enemy of God, taking away the merits of any good actions and depriving us of the right to everlasting happiness in heaven.

Every mortal sin that can be recalled after diligent examination of conscience must be told to a priest in confession before a person is free to receive Holy Communion again. It's not the kind of sin to gloss over. Because mortal sin literally blocks God's love and cuts us off from receiving grace, a penitent must be sure to tell the priest in confession in order for the sacrament to be valid and the person's soul restored to a state of grace. An important caution: If I *forget* to confess a mortal sin and remember it later, my previous confession was valid, but the forgotten sin must still be confessed.

I don't believe that young children can very easily commit a mortal sin because of their innocence and the fact that the Church teaches that in order for any person, young or old, to commit such a sin three things must be present: (1) It must be a serious matter. (2) There must be sufficient reflection; in other words, the person must have considered the seriousness of the sin. (3) Full consent of the will must be given.

The best way we parents can help our children develop a proper formation of conscience and a devotion to the sacrament of penance is to frequently receive the sacrament ourselves — preferably *with them.*

Let your kids know:

● The more often we go to confession, the more grace God can pour into our souls. Grace increases willpower to withstand temptations.

● No sin, no matter how habit-forming it has become, will ever get an unbreakable hold on us, so long as we keep going to confession and seeking God's help and grace.

● Confession once a month is a good rule of thumb. Unless a serious sin (mortal sin) has been committed, which should be confessed as soon as possible, the routine of frequent reception of the sacrament of reconciliation keeps us aware of our shortcomings, our need for forgiveness, and the love of a merciful God.

● The sacrament of penance is a means of restoring our friendship with God, thereby offering us a greater peace with our brothers and sisters and bestowing a greater peace within our heart.

Jesus said to his apostles: " 'Peace be with you. As the Father has sent me, even so I send you.' When he had said this, he breathed on them and said to them, 'Receive the Holy Spirit. If you forgive the sins of any, they are forgiven them; if you retain the sins of any, they are retained' " (John 20:21-23).

Again, the Church offers parents and their children all the help necessary to stay in the state of grace and resist temptation. Prayer and frequent reception of the sacraments act as tools, helping to build our faith and bringing us closer to God.

Sometimes even good people can begin to believe they don't have enough strength to fight off all the temptations that surround them. Kind of like the old phrase "The devil made me do it" — we end up excusing ourselves for our weakness!

Nice try, but we Christians who believe know better. That's like doubting God and saying his grace is *not working.* Something's not working, all right; but we can't blame God. It's us — every time we fail to act in cooperation with the grace he offers.

In addition to prayer and frequent reception of the sacraments, I like to remind my children often:

● Remember that your guardian angel is always with you.

● Keep in mind that your body is a temple of the Holy Spirit.

● Keep busy. When you are active, in work and in play — and this includes time each day doing physical work and play — you are less likely to have the energy or inclination to sin.

● Say "no" to yourself, just as soon as the sinful thought pops into your head.

● Avoid the "occasions of sin" — those people, places, and things that you know will entice you to do wrong.

Sometimes our children don't know where to begin, or what to confess. While this sacrament is a very personal and intimate gift between the priest and the penitent, we can help our young make a good confession by our own example and by offering them guidelines.

And on the occasions when I detect a few balkers in the group, I offer my generic "If there's anyone here who thinks he or she is perfect and doesn't need to go to confession today, see me. I'll be glad to make you a list." In reality, they could probably do a better number on me and my faults than I could on them.

We want to remind our children to be adequately prepared before going into the confessional. One of my more hyper teens could make the block-and-a-half walk, confess his sins, say his penance, and be in the back door before the other kids had left the house. I was *not* pleased, and I'll bet the poor priest is still trying to figure out what the kid told him!

I have now gotten in the habit of reminding my children to take a few minutes to think over what it is they have done (or failed to do) that displeased God and hurt others. Rehearsing their sins to themselves a couple of times is a healthy reminder of what it is they need to work on.

They should also rehearse the Act of Contrition so that they can recite it properly and meaningfully. Most importantly, they must take time to stay and say the penance the priest gives them (unless it is a penance to be done at another time). In addition, they should spend at least a few minutes in thanksgiving for God's generous love. This is the time they should ask themselves what it is they can do to improve their relationship to God and to others.

God does not expect us to remember each and every venial sin or the number of times committed. Being honest, sincere, and sorry with a firm purpose of amendment is what's important. We all need the grace that comes to us in confession. It's key to helping us avoid those sins in the future.

With that in mind, the following is offered as a brief guide for an examination of conscience:

THE TEN COMMANDMENTS

1 ● I, THE LORD, AM YOUR GOD. YOU SHALL NOT HAVE OTHER GODS BESIDES ME. Have I failed to show my love for God? Do I pray? Have I denied my faith or its beliefs? Have I read books or participated in something that was against the Catholic Church? Have I believed or participated in superstitious, cultic, or satanic practices (fortunetelling, lucky charms, omens, etc.)?

2 ● YOU SHALL NOT TAKE THE NAME OF THE LORD, YOUR GOD, IN VAIN. Did I curse or swear? Did I set a bad example by my cursing (particularly if I used God's name) in the presence of others who may be scandalized by my behavior? Did I speak against the Church or a Church leader? Did I speak irreverently about the Church, her saints, her practices, customs, or traditions? Did I join a forbidden society — one that denies or denigrates the Catholic faith?

3 ● REMEMBER TO KEEP HOLY THE SABBATH DAY. Have I missed Mass through my own fault? Do I come late or leave early, without a good reason? Do I show reverence for Sundays by avoiding unnecessary work?

4 ● HONOR YOUR FATHER AND YOUR MOTHER. Do I obey my parents and other lawful superiors? Do I show them proper respect? Have I talked back, used disrespectful language, or failed to be considerate and helpful in the home? Have I done things to grieve my parents or to make them unhappy? Do I spend time with my family?

5 ● YOU SHALL NOT KILL. Have I abused my body or that of another? Have I misused food, alcoholic drink, or drugs? Did I give or sell illegal drugs or chemicals to another? Did I harbor anger, resentment, or hatred toward another? Did I fight, give bad example, or cause others to be uncharitable or hateful toward another? Was my language malicious or hate-inspiring? Did I unjustly strike or hurt another? Did I endanger another's life or health? Did I forgive those who have hurt me? Did I lead others into sin or to commit sin? Did I submit to or cause or encourage another to have an abortion? Have I shown indifference to or condoned abortion or euthanasia (mercy killing)?

6 ● YOU SHALL NOT COMMIT ADULTERY. Have I been chaste (decent and pure) in my thoughts, words, and actions? Have I read impure (erotic) books, magazines, or papers or offered them to others? Have I watched impure movies or videos? Was I modest in my dress and behavior? Have I spoken of impure things (including jokes or stories)? Have I been the occasion of sin for another because of my words, dress, or indecent actions? Am I guilty of dating someone who is not free to marry? Did I consent to passionate kissing, fondling, and other sexually arousing actions (such as touching forbidden areas) outside of marriage? Am I guilty of masturbation (impurity with self, that is, erotic self-stimulation), fornication (sexual intercourse before marriage), adultery (sexual intercourse with a married person other than my spouse), or birth control (the Pill or other means that would prevent an openness to new life)?

7 ● YOU SHALL NOT STEAL. Have I stolen anything from another, from an employer, or failed to pay just taxes? Have I returned those stolen items or offered compensation for what was taken? Have I damaged another's property? Have I been excessively stingy toward my family or to the Church? Did I charge inflated or exorbitant prices for my goods or services? Did I cheat or deprive employees or others of their just wages? Have I cheated in other ways, such as in games of chance? Gambled excessively? Was I lazy in my work around the home, in my study habits, or have I failed to do sufficient work for the wages paid to me at my job?

8 ● YOU SHALL NOT BEAR FALSE WITNESS AGAINST YOUR NEIGH- BOR. Have I gossiped or lied? Have I slandered another? Have I revealed confidences or secrets I shouldn't have divulged? Have I been uncharitable or unjustly or overly critical in what I say or discuss? Have I encouraged others to slander or to talk ill of another and thereby hurt or ruin that person's reputation? Have I wrongfully suspected or judged others?

9 ● YOU SHALL NOT COVET YOUR NEIGHBOR'S WIFE [HUSBAND]. Have I consented to sexually arousing thoughts and fan- tasies about someone to whom I am not married? Have I in- dulged in pornography in the form of books and magazines or movies and videos? Have I failed to direct my thoughts and imagination away from impure (erotic) matters, praying for help to remove such thoughts in times of weakness?

10 ● YOU SHALL NOT COVET YOUR NEIGHBOR'S GOODS. Have I been greedy and selfish? Have I been envious of another? Have I jealously desired property that belongs to others? Do I concentrate too much on material accomplishments or material gain?

* * *

As Catholics we know that in order to receive absolution for our sins we must confess them to a priest, be sorry for our sins, and make a firm resolution not to sin again and to avoid those occasions we know to be sinful.

One of the requirements of the sacrament of penance (reconciliation) is saying an Act of Contrition, of which there are several versions, among them:

ACT OF CONTRITION (**Traditional**) ✝ O my God, I am heartily sorry for having offended you. I detest all my sins because of your just punishments, but most of all because they offend you, my God, who are all good and deserving of all my love. I firmly resolve, with the help of your grace, to sin no more and to avoid the occasions of sin. Amen.

PENITENT'S ACT OF SORROW (Contemporary) ✝ My God, I am sorry for my sins with all my heart. In choosing to do wrong and failing to do good, I have sinned against you, whom I should love above all things. I firmly intend, with your help, to do penance, to sin no more, and to avoid whatever leads me to sin. Our Savior, Jesus Christ, suffered and died for us. In his name, my God, have mercy. Amen.

IN CASE OF EMERGENCY OR IMMINENT DEATH ✝ Dear God, I am sorry for all my sins. Please forgive me. Amen.

17

❦

Childlike Concepts of Heaven, Hell, and Purgatory

My kids, like most believing Christians, have their own imaginative idea of heaven. Kari, our creative then eight-year-old drew a picture of a huge angel complete with halo, wings, and outstretched arms balancing on top of a golden gate. On the other side was a flowered path with little angels who welcome newcomers to a huge castle she labeled "God's house." At the time she drew the picture, she said there was a sandbox, a park, and paints to play with inside!

Angela, a more "street-wise" ten, pictured God sitting in a king-size easy chair dressed in a T-shirt and slacks with an angel on each side of him. Her concept of heaven then was a place full of "friends, toys, Mom and Dad, family, and animals to play with."

Like Kari and Angela, each one of us has an image of what we think heaven might be or, perhaps, what we'd *like* it to be. Though a truth of our faith, heaven is also a mystery.

There are all sorts of theological rationalizations to explain heaven, hell, and even purgatory. But how do we say it in lay terms — or more importantly — how do we teach it to our kids?

While heaven is often described as the "place or state of perfect happiness," hell is the absence of such happiness. In heaven the saints share fully in God's life and love. They are perfectly united with him and can never lose him.

On the other hand, the Church warns of the reality of hell. Scripture speaks plainly of eternal punishment for grave and unrepented sin, and warns against the deliberate malice that corrupts the person from within and leads to eternal death.

We've all met those who claim, "I really don't believe that hell exists. After all, God is all-merciful. He'd never condemn anyone — no matter how bad — to eternal damnation."

We must not be deceived; therefore, let's keep the following in mind:

● Remember *who* we're dealing with here! It is no less than Satan, the father of lies, and he would like nothing better than to convince us that there's no such place as hell. All the while he's working feverishly to get us there!

● To deny hell is to deny the gift of free will that God gave to each person. We are free to choose God and reject the selfishness of sin just as we are free to choose hell if that is what we desire. God, though he may "hound" us like he does in Francis Thompson's *Hound of Heaven*, will never force his love on us.

● God is certainly "all merciful," but we must never forget that he is also "all just," and it will be that justice by which we are judged at death.

● When Christ spoke of hell, he spoke in compassion, to warn us: "But when the Son of Man comes in his glory, and all the angels with him, then he will sit on the throne of his glory. All the nations will be gathered before him, and he will separate people one from another as a shepherd separates the sheep from the goats, and he will put the sheep at his right. . . . Then the king will say to those at his right hand, 'Come, you that are blessed by my Father, inherit the kingdom prepared for you from the foundation of the world'; . . . Then he will say to those at his left hand, 'You that are accursed, depart from me into the eternal fire prepared for the devil and his angels'; . . . And these will go away into eternal punishment, but the righteous into eternal life" (Matthew 25:31-34, 41, 46). The Old Testament, too, spoke of life after death: "Many of those who sleep in the dust of the earth shall awake, some to everlasting life, and some to share an everlasting contempt" (Daniel 12:2). We are also told that "the souls of the righteous are in the hand of God, and no torment will ever touch them. In the eyes of the foolish they seemed to have died, . . . but they are at peace. For though in the sight of others they were punished, their hope is full of immortality" (Wisdom of Solomon 3:1-4).

My mother often loved to repeat the story of her discussion of heaven with our Vietnamese-born adopted son, Tony, which took place when he was a curious four-year-old. She told him that God created each of us and we were all to be part of his divine plan. "Just think, Tony. God planned you, and you were up in heaven in God's mind before you were born and before you came to America and to your mommy and daddy."

"I know," Tony matter-of-factly replied.

"Well, God planned each one of us. And, guess what? I was once in heaven, too. . ." Grandma began to explain about her own beginnings.

Tony interrupted quickly and excitedly asked, "You were in heaven, too? Well, I didn't see you there!" From the mouths of babes. . . .

As to purgatory, my good friend Mike Fleming, who is a convert to the faith, has a cute and commonsense concept: "All the other religions talk about heaven and hell in such black-and-white terms. You're either saved or you're not. It's heaven or it's hell with them. There's no room for an 'in-between.' And there's no gray area for those who aren't bad enough for hell but sure aren't good enough to go straight to heaven. That's what I like about the Catholic Church. They believe in a gray area. In case you're not quite ready for heaven there's a purgatory to help you get ready. It makes you feel like you've got a fighting chance if you weren't always perfect!"

Mike's theory may not measure up to the theories of the theological greats, yet even the late Bishop Fulton J. Sheen, world-renowned speaker, author, and television personality, used to rhetorically ask, "Is there any one of us — no matter how saintly — who believes he or she is really worthy to meet God face to face and not need a little time to stop and prepare for such a meeting?"

Death, Bishop Sheen suggests, is like an unexpected houseguest. As welcome as the guest may be, we'd like to take a moment to make sure the house is clean, our hair is combed, and we are ready to enjoy the visit.

It kind of reminded me of the wonderful surprise party my daughter Chrissy and my good friend Dorothy planned in honor of our twenty-fifth wedding anniversary. When friends began to arrive, my husband, John, was taking a nap; and I, in a grubby short outfit, had just sat down after bathing a batch of dirty kids who had been playing in a sandbox. John and I were surprised all right!

The Catholic Catechism explains purgatory as "the place or state of those who have died in grace, but burdened by venial sins and imperfections, or before they have done suitable penance for their sins. In purgatory they are cleansed of these last hindrances to their entry into the vision of God."

It is believed that at the time of death, the soul will realize far more than it could before the infinite goodness of God. It will then suffer, knowing that it is for a while blocked from the beatific vision by the obstacles (sins) of its own making.

St. Augustine says that the suffering of purgatory is more severe than any earthly suffering. Yet those in purgatory have also a radical peace, for they are now sure of salvation, and know that God wills this "purgation" out of his great love for them.

We may not be able to adequately explain to our young the mystery of heaven, hell, purgatory, or eternal life — after all, it's a mystery to us, too. The point we want to get across to our kids is that God in his magnificence — and from the beginning of time — knew all, planned all, and designed a purpose and role for each of us to play in this divine plan.

Living in an age of legal abortion, we must continually remind our young that God makes no mistakes, and in his eyes each one of us, no matter our age, race, or condition, is planned and wanted for a unique purpose that only we can serve.

We also want them to know that when we choose to do good, we are fulfilling the plan God has for our lives. In fact, God will supply all the graces we need to resist evil and choose good.

"Is Grandma K with Jesus up in heaven now that she's dead?" was the first question out of our children's mouths after their beloved grandmother died.

"Dad and I sure think she is in heaven and probably having all kinds of fun. And, I'll bet, too, she's got her eye on you guys and will be praying for you. Grandma is now part of the common union [communion] of saints. If she's not yet in heaven, she's at a 'stopping-off place' called purgatory."

We want our kids to know they now have Grandma — "our own personal Kuharski saint" — to whom they can turn and pray when they need special favors or help.

We, like most parents, have witnessed the death of close loved ones and friends. These occasions, sad as they usually are, are timely opportunities to teach our children about the importance of praying *for* and *to* those who have died.

In fact, from early centuries, prayers for "the faithful departed" were encouraged and Mass was offered for them. Aware of the bonds that link us with those who have died in Christ, the Church never ceases to remember and pray for the departed.

The Church teaches that the communion of saints is the union of love and spiritual help that binds together all those who belong to Christ: the faithful living on earth, the blessed in heaven, and those suffering in purgatory. According to Vatican II's *Dogmatic Constitution on the Church*, our union with those we love "who have gone to sleep in the peace of Christ is not in the least interrupted."

Our family recently attended the funeral Mass of another dear friend. Ed was only fifty-six and died within six weeks of being diagnosed with inoperable brain cancer.

Our kids remembered Ed for the magic tricks, stories, and fun times they had on his hobby farm. John and I recalled our friendship with Ed and his wife, Jane, and our mutual involvement with pro-life concerns. When I told a priest-friend about our family's shock and sorrow over Ed's sudden death, and the loss he would be to our social justice concerns, he gently reminded me, "He will be more helpful to you now than ever."

Father was right: Ed would now become part of the Mystical Body of Christ known as the communion of saints. The saints in heaven intercede for us; we pray for those in purgatory; the ties of love bind together all the members of Christ until the final resurrection and the final judgment when all will be made perfect in God. At every Mass offered, there is a special time to recall and pray for those loved ones who have died.

"Grandma K, Ed, and all of our other departed friends are part of the Mystical Body of Christ because they were baptized Christians who loved God when they lived in this world," we tell our young.

When Grandma K died, our whole family cried and mourned her loss. Of course, we believe in life after death and that she was heaven-bound. But our emotions were a normal human reaction. We would miss her terribly. In these circumstances it is good and healthy to let our children know that it is all right to cry.

Yet what a powerful thought and special consolation to know we have Grandma K and other "friends in high places" who will be pleading our case, and to whom we can turn for help in our effort to love God and do his will.

When it comes to teaching our children about heaven, hell, and purgatory, we take our cue from an old show tune: "Accentuate the positive and eliminate the negative."

There are two simple yet important prayers to say for friends or loved ones who have died. They are:

✝

Eternal rest grant unto them, O Lord, and let perpetual light shine upon them. May they rest in peace. Amen.

✝

May her/his soul, and all the souls of the faithful departed, rest in peace. Amen.

18

❦

Corporal Works of Mercy Help Get the Job Done

How often have you taken your children along when you attended a wake or funeral, visited a sick friend, helped a neighbor or brought a hot dish to someone who lives alone? Well, each one of these acts is considered by the Church to be a corporal work of mercy *if done* in the name of Christ for the love of God (see Matthew 25:34-40). Each one of these everyday deeds can become our best tools to teach our children about the love of God and neighbor.

Sometimes we Christians worry about how to teach faith and values to our young. In an age saturated by secular humanistic "me-first" attitudes, there is certainly cause for concern. But when we use the spiritual "technology" the Church offers — the sacraments and prayer — and we consciously practice the corporal and spiritual works of mercy, we've "got it made." More importantly, so do our kids!

It's vital to let our children know that a person's greatness — *saintliness* — comes not only from the noble, courageous, or spectacularly obvious deeds but also from simple, seemingly insignificant acts performed for the honor and glory of God.

One of my favorite saints, St. Thérèse of Lisieux, entered the Carmelite convent at a very young age (fifteen) and died at the age of twenty-four. Yet she became known as one of the greatest saints of contemporary times — not for her heroic deeds but for the simple acts she performed heroically.

In fact, her assigned job in the cloistered convent was *laundress*. Now this is a saint I can relate to! You want to talk "heroic"? She did her laundering before the invention of the automatic washer and dryer!

St. Thérèse wrote in her diary, "I was not like those grand souls who practice all kinds of penances from childhood. My mortification consisted in checking my self-will, keeping back an impatient word, doing little things for those around me without their knowing it, and countless things like that."

For Thérèse, "holiness consists of a disposition of the heart which makes us small and humble in the arms of God, aware of our weakness, yet confident — boldly confident — in the goodness of our Father."

Our kids may never hear about the corporal and spiritual works of mercy from anyone else: not "on the street," not from a friend, or perhaps not even in a religious or school setting. So it's up to us to tell them. After all, the Church teaches that it is we parents who are the *primary* educators of our children.

The seven corporal works of mercy are (1) to feed the hungry, (2) to give drink to the thirsty, (3) to clothe the naked, (4) to visit the imprisoned, (5) to shelter the homeless, (6) to visit the sick, and (7) to bury the dead.

Parents shouldn't be reluctant about reminding their children of simple occasions to do good.

I've decided that perhaps one of the greatest gifts I can give my kids is *not* to make it too easy for them. In other words, I try to offer them a healthy measure of love mixed with discipline (love in another form), and then pray for opportunities in which they, too, can perform little works of mercy.

When children are very young, this may mean nothing more spectacular than doing their homework, taking out the garbage, washing the kitchen floor, cleaning the pet rat's cage (oh, the likes of what some of us contend with!), cutting Grandma's grass, or keeping their room clean without grumbling.

Yet the occasions in our adult life that call for kindness are often equally modest. All of us face opportunities each and every day to practice one or more corporal works of mercy.

1 ● TO FEED THE HUNGRY. God calls some to join the Peace Corps or similar organization, to become active missionaries in foreign lands, or to volunteer in soup kitchens. (Running your own *does* count!)

For those of us who are stay-at-home moms, however, nursing the baby, preparing tasty meals for the family, setting an attractive table, or inviting someone who is alone over for dinner can be a source of grace and a corporal work of mercy.

For my husband and undoubtedly many others, it may be nothing more grand than bypassing temptations to self-indulgence in order to provide for the family. In times of great need, a husband may be called upon to take on supplemental work in order that his wife has the opportunity to remain in the home to nurture their young children. Certainly, this would be a sacrifice on both of their parts and a corporal work of mercy.

Offering to help with the parish food collection, and even the tedious tasks of grocery shopping, cooking, and doing dishes are all works of mercy if done with the right intention.

Training our children to set the table "WG" (without grumbling), to share a treat occasionally, or to go without — in order to put in their own offering for the parish food and clothing drive — are great ways to involve them in the family's good works.

This reminds me of the time our Chrissy, then an eager kindergartner, saved a cookie she had earned in school and carried the fragile goodie on the long bus ride and walk home in order to share it with her three young brothers and sisters — not because she knew it was a corporal work of mercy but "just 'cuz I wanted them to have a taste of the M&M's on top." I'm not sure if it falls exactly under the heading of "mercy," but it surely was *love*.

2 ● TO GIVE DRINK TO THE THIRSTY. Food and drink sustain the body, so our efforts in seeing that others are not deprived can be acts of love and mercy, which brings to mind Ted and Dorothy Hustead, owners and founders of the famous Wall Drug in South Dakota. As the story goes, the Husteads, both Catholics, owned a pharmacy that was attracting few of the busy vacation travelers who drove Interstate 90 to get to their various destinations, including the Badlands, Mount

Rushmore, and the Black Hills. One day Ted, at Dorothy's prompting, put up a few simple signs along the highway offering "Free Water" and "Ice Water."

One might suggest it was a brilliant sales gimmick because, over the years, the Husteads' little drugstore turned into a million-dollar enterprise featuring a shopping mall, restaurants, art exhibits, concessions, shops, and lodging. But the fact remains that the blessings (and profits) came to the Husteads only *after* they offered the free drinking water.

The Church teaches that it is an act of love and mercy to help others to obtain nourishment, especially those in great need. In a real sense that is what Ted and Dorothy Hustead did for those passersby in South Dakota.

The Church encourages us to never neglect the needs of others. When we know of others — whether in our own community or in foreign lands — who suffer because they lack the basic necessities of life, we are required to be generous and committed in our effort to relieve their suffering because Christ calls us to do so.

3 ● TO CLOTHE THE NAKED. Participating in parish clothing drives, sending money or goods to the missions, or passing along your own clothing to others in your community are more obvious acts of mercy.

In a less noticeable way, mercy is also expressed through the minutes and hours we spend washing, mending, and sewing clothes for our family. All of these acts of service can become tokens of love to God and to others just by our mere intention.

Asking our children to hang, fold, or iron clothes (I remind them to "offer it up" when they groan and say "It's not my turn"), or to dress the baby can likewise be a means of grace and an act of love for them.

4 ● TO VISIT THE IMPRISONED. Besides the obvious practices of visiting those in jail or writing to them, we can offer comfort to many in today's world who feel trapped or imprisoned by circumstances that surround them: the elderly relative who can no longer get around; the sickly neighbor down the block; someone — old or young — who needs assistance in getting to the grocery store or library; a child who needs baby-sitting or those who need street patrols in order to cross busy inter-sections safely. Again the key is attempting to see Christ in each person we serve.

5 ● TO SHELTER THE HOMELESS. Simple acts of dusting, clean-ing, pitching in around the house, and taking good care of our home and surroundings can be a source of grace in the spirit of St. Thérèse. (I'm not exactly sure under what category "cleaning the pet white rat's cage" falls, but I'll use any angle to get the job done.)

The concept of sheltering the homeless extends outward to include (in my estimation) lawn-mowing, shoveling, or paint-ing (without expecting financial reward) for a loved one or neighbor who can no longer perform these functions.

Referring to the corporal works of mercy, Christ reminds us that "just as you did not do it to one of the least of these, you did not do it to me" (Matthew 25:45). In other words, whenever we neglect the least in our own little kingdom, we are neglecting Christ. With that in mind we must never be smug about our circumstances or forget about those less for-tunate who count on our kindness in order to be clothed, cared for, and sheltered.

6 ● TO VISIT THE SICK. Running errands for those who are ill, spending some time visiting, reading to them, or helping to do a task they're unable to tackle are a few of the ways we can perform this corporal work of mercy.

There is an obvious antilife climate that has permeated all of today's society. Some 1.6 million preborn babies (one every twenty seconds) are killed by abortion every year; and there is a not-so-subtle drive to extend the killing by euthanasia to the elderly, sick, and most vulnerable.

We may never be personally responsible for restoring legal protection to the preborn child, or in eliminating the dis-crimination that threatens the lives and rights of others who are vulnerable and defenseless. But our acts of goodness — even if no one sees or seems to appreciate them — can do much to kindle a spark of Christianity that ignites others to action.

Speaking as one working on the "home front," I believe we must not underestimate the power of our actions. Children imitate what they *see* from us, far more than any lectures or outside influences. Perhaps the most pro-life example we set is to welcome a new baby into our family, care for a neighbor or loved one, or take the time to visit the sick (including the crabby and ungrateful).

7 ● **TO BURY THE DEAD.** No one *enjoys* attending wakes or funerals, but if you have ever lost a loved one in death, you will remember how comforted you were by those who took the time to stop by with a gift of food, fresh flowers, or attended the wake or funeral with you.

The Church teaches us to show respect for the bodies of the dead and the places in which they are buried. Thus, visiting a grave site, saying prayers for the dead person, cutting the grass and pulling weeds around the grave are all acts of love if done in Christ's name.

My uncle Don was known for his habit of going to the wakes of relatives, friends, and even co-workers. We kids used to wonder just how many he attended in a month. When he died, his family found memorial cards in the breast pocket of his suits, and, as my cousin Diane described it, "a stack thicker than a deck of cards" in his dresser drawer.

What an example to his children! And what a wonderful way to be remembered, as one who took the time to console and comfort those in mourning.

Practicing any or all of the seven corporal works of mercy is not only an act of friendship and support to others but is our heavenly Father's way of bringing us closer to him.

19

❦

Spiritual Works of Mercy

Most Christian parents in the "trenches" know only too well that it's far more difficult to take the time to correct or straighten out a wayward kid than to "let it go." So, too, does it consume more patience and energy to instill in our children faith, morals, and manners; to offer a listening ear (tired though it may be); or to forgive someone who has hurt us.

Well, all of these things are considered spiritual works of mercy and can be sources of grace if done for the love of God and neighbor. Another try at that unruly kid might almost be inviting!

Actually, we may not hear much about the spiritual works of mercy, but the Church considers them by definition to be "acts of love toward others to help them in the needs of their souls." And since the soul is more important than the body, the spiritual works of mercy are even more important than the corporal works of mercy.

The seven spiritual works of mercy are (1) to admonish the sinner, (2) to instruct the ignorant, (3) to counsel the doubtful, (4) to comfort the sorrowful, (5) to bear wrongs patiently, (6) to forgive all injuries, and (7) to pray for the living and the dead.

So how can we apply this to our everyday lives as laypeople regardless of whether or not we're trying to pass on the faith to our young as parents in the "trenches"? Well, I don't have all the answers, but a little of my own hands-on experience mixed with Church teaching might suggest some ideas.

1 ● TO ADMONISH THE SINNER. The Church considers it an act of love when we help another realize the seriousness of sin or to warn another about situations that may be occasions of sin.

You don't have to be a parent to accomplish this. Grandparent, godparent, caring friend, or confidant will do. Setting a good example, going to Mass and confession frequently, encouraging others (especially the young) to do the same, and reminding them of God's love and forgiveness are all considered spiritual works of mercy.

Oftentimes, we Catholics are far too complacent about the role models we are to those around us. I still remember the young man who came to talk with me after I gave a pro-life presentation at his college campus.

"If it hadn't been for my best buddy in high school, my life might have been so much different. I might have made some very bad — dreadful — decisions," he confided.

It seems this young guy was getting quite serious with a girl he was dating. "One day my buddy pulled me aside and said, 'Look, if you two don't watch out, you're going to end up in deep trouble,'" the young man said. "We had quite a talk. What he said took real courage. And love! I owe that guy a lot."

The friend, instead of urging his buddy toward sexual promiscuity, gently but firmly reminded him of the physical and moral dangers involved. A spiritual work of mercy and "peer pressure" at its best!

2 ● TO INSTRUCT THE IGNORANT. The Church says it is an act of love to help others to learn the truths they need to know to save their souls. In addition to taking the time to teach our children properly, we are compelled to be positive role models for them and for those who see us as authority figures.

This particular spiritual work brought to mind a recent "Ann Landers" column written about parents who were guest panelists on television. Their "claim to fame" was that they all believed in allowing their teens and young adults to have "sex at home with their dates" because it was a "safer environment" preferable to backseats in parked cars or other more potentially dangerous surroundings. Talk about a moral copout! Sad to say, the moral corruption these parents have wreaked upon their young may take generations to undo.

In sharp contrast are those parents who refuse to "let the schools do it," negating their roles as the primary teachers of their children. In spite of the present "safe sex" culture or "values neutral" sex education, many Christians today are living witnesses to their children and members of the community by the moral lifestyle and leadership they offer. The Church reminds us that each of us has the potential to teach others about our faith and the love of God.

3 ● TO COUNSEL THE DOUBTFUL. It is an act of love to help others to be certain about what they should do to love and serve God. This could mean anything from reassuring our youngsters — especially during the sensitive teen and young adult years — to offering a listening ear to a friend or acquaintance.

Julie, over a casual lunch one day, confided to Liz about the emotional roller coaster she was on: "I should be happy. Financially we're pretty secure. The kids are in school, doing well, and are involved in all sorts of fun extracurricular projects. And John and I just returned from a great vacation. So why am I not happy? What's causing these persistent headaches?"

When Liz asked if she'd seen a good doctor, Julie described the numerous physical and psychological exams she had undergone, not to mention the specialists she had consulted.

After listening to what seemed like an endless litany of medical opinion, Liz remembered that Julie was living in an invalid second marriage. Before she had a chance to consider it as being "out of line," she bluntly asked, "Julie, when was the last time you went to confession?"

Softening her voice, Julie responded that she and her family went weekly to Mass but because she *assumed* her marriage would not be recognized in the eyes of the Church, it had been years since she had gone to confession or Communion.

"Don't assume where God is involved. Just go talk it over with a priest," Liz urged.

Two days later, Julie called Liz. "Father Tom spent two hours with me. He was so receptive, and I have *you* to thank for getting me there!"

Several months later Father Tom performed a short service blessing Julie and John's marriage. Liz and her husband were honored to witness the event! Liz, perhaps without fully being aware at the time, had counseled the doubtful and brought her back into the fullness of the faith. (Needless to say, Julie's headaches and doctor calls ceased.)

4 ● TO COMFORT THE SORROWFUL. It is an act of love to help another person in any kind of sorrow and to refrain from doing anything that would unnecessarily cause a person more sorrow.

Anyone who has ever sat and listened to a confused or hurting heart knows that it often takes buckets of time, energy, and maybe even patience. It's probably easier to send a check in the mail to a mission in Africa! Yet God presents each one of us with numerous occasions when we can be a source of love and comfort to another. The trick is seeing ourselves as Christ's ambassador and using the opportunity the way God wants us to.

Being there for someone who recently lost a loved one in death, consoling a mother who recently suffered a miscarriage, offering a shoulder to someone victimized by chemical abuse or abandonment, or simply comforting a hurting child or jilted teen attempting to recover from a soured puppy love are a few ways to practice this spiritual work of mercy.

5 ● TO BEAR WRONGS PATIENTLY. It is an act of love to accept the consequences of another's thoughtlessness or carelessness and to suffer inconveniences that another should bear. This spiritual work calls us to sainthood by not only urging us to accept the results of our own actions but to bear the faults of others with love and patience!

Wow! How's that for a tall order? Whenever I think my faith life is going well, I remember this one.

As for accepting injuries: Since Eve excused her part in the original sin by blaming the serpent, all human beings tend to put the blame on another or attempt to "even the score" when they feel they've been wronged.

The story of Mother Teresa of Calcutta, and her effort to see her dying mother one last time, is an outstanding example of "bearing the wrongs of others." The Albanian Embassy repeatedly refused her visa request, and no amount of diplomatic intervention by influential statesmen including U Thant (then Secretary General of the United Nations) and others could persuade the Albanian government differently.

According to David Porter's *Mother Teresa, the Early Years*, on one occasion as the nun left the Albanian Embassy with tears in her eyes, she looked up toward heaven and said, "Oh, God, I understand and accept my own sufferings. But it is hard to understand and accept my mother's, when all she desires in her old age is to see us again."

In spite of her sorrow, Mother Teresa accepted the situation and so, too, did her mother who later wrote, "Even if we never meet again in this sad world we shall surely meet in heaven."

Urging our children to resist the urge to "strike back" against a thoughtless playmate or to practice more patience toward an annoying brother or sister will help set them on a course that offers grace and far more satisfaction than any temporary retaliation.

6 ● TO FORGIVE ALL INJURIES. It is an act of deep love to forgive all those who have injured us in any way — even deliberately. Christ demands that his followers have great love and forgiveness for one another in imitation of his own forgiveness of his enemies as he hung on the cross.

You may recall the story in Chapter 2 of how our adopted black/Cambodian son, Charlie, was picked on (along with one of our natural sons, Tim) by older boys and called demeaning names. Despite how he was treated, Charlie later offered a prayer for their detractors. Well, when Charlie was twelve, he had a similar experience. He was on his paper route several blocks from our home when two older and bigger boys grabbed his newspapers, scattered them, then started punching and kicking him and calling him "nigger."

I was (fortunately or unfortunately) seven months pregnant at the time; otherwise, I would've chased down those hoodlums and heaven knows what I would've done to them! I called the police, but they were unable to find the culprits. At any rate, to make a long story short, Charlie once again taught our family a beautiful lesson about bearing wrongs and forgiving injuries by suggesting at dinnertime prayer that we "say an extra one for those boys because they don't know any better." If that isn't a spiritual work of mercy, I don't what is!

7 ● TO PRAY FOR THE LIVING AND THE DEAD. As believing Christians, we are members of the Mystical Body of Christ and part of the communion of saints. When we pray for those on earth or those who have died, we are truly spreading the fires of love to others whether in this world or in purgatory.

One of the examples I am most grateful to my adoptive parents and family for is their reverence for life and the dead. I don't remember a Memorial Day that we didn't pack up rakes, garden equipment, and even the lawn mower, and visit the grave sites of relatives where we cleaned, cut, and then prayed over the headstone of each one. Most had died before my adoption into the family, but the annual demonstration taught me much about my parents' faith and love of family.

Equally memorable were the many wakes and funerals I attended with my parents as a youngster. Seeing them consoling and comforting others, sending a bouquet of flowers, having a Mass said, bringing over a dish of food to the bereaved family — these were common responses in my family. I want my children to have the same memories.

Living in an age when legalized abortion so callously threatens the lives of preborn babies and witnessing a growing drive toward active euthanasia of the elderly, sick, and vulnerable should make us realize that this spiritual work of praying for the living and the dead should be integrated as part of our everyday prayer lives.

In summary, God gives us opportunities in abundance to perform many spiritual works of mercy. The only requirement is that they be done for the love of God and neighbor. In essence, we are really loving Christ by loving the members of his Mystical Body. He himself said, "Truly I tell you, just as you did it to one of the least of these who are members of my family, you did it to me" (Matthew 25:40).

THE TEN COMANDMENTS

1. I, the Lord, am your god. You shall not have other gods besides me.

ruler

He is not a ruler

2. You shall not take the name of god in vain.

Don't say that word!

3. Remember to keep the holy sabbath day.

4. Honor your father and mother.

5. You shall not kill.

Don't kill me!

By Kari Kuharski Age 9

20

❦

What Are the Precepts, or Commandments, of the Church?

Several years ago Minnesota joined the growing list of states that offer a lottery. "Buy one ticket and you just may become that million-dollar-plus winner!" Wouldn't we all rush out to get that ticket if we knew it was a sure win? Yet oddsmakers warn that a person has a better chance of "being struck by lightning" than winning the state lottery.

Odds aside, since the lottery came to town, people of all ages and incomes line up regularly at the local gas station, grocery store, and pharmacy to buy tickets. Oh, that there were as much enthusiasm and persistence about our spiritual lives!

Catholics have a surefire ticket to heaven with no lottery, guesswork, or risk-taking involved. And the reward is nothing less than everlasting life and happiness. A billion-dollar lottery win is as nothing by comparison.

Yet the faith life of many of today's culture-caught Christians is performed by rote or shelved altogether, only to be revived during times of disaster and crisis. We can easily be consumed by such a "me-first" climate unless we make a concerted, prayerful, and *daily* effort to put Christ — and not culture — first.

This is all the more important to do if we are parents. After all, children generally will imitate not what we say but what they see us do.

The Church teaches that the basic vocation of every Christian is to love God and to love others: "You shall love the Lord your God with all your heart, and with all your soul, and with all your strength, and with all your mind; and your neighbor as yourself" (Luke 10:27).

We want our children to know that God has a plan and a purpose for each one of us and that he calls us to live out that vocation in such a way so as to give glory to him and service to others: "Now there are varieties of gifts, but the same Spirit; and there are varieties of services, but the same Lord" (1 Corinthians 12:4-5).

As parents we take on another serious obligation. It is our duty to love, care for, and educate our children. In fact, we are viewed by the Church (and the State) as the primary educators of our young. This means we can't push the obligation off on others — even if they are instructors in Catholic schools.

I will never forget my shock when my son Tim, then an average fun-loving nineteen-year-old, waltzed in one Friday night to tell me he was going camping and fishing with buddies for the weekend. When I asked where he would be attending Sunday Mass, he casually replied, "Oh, I'll probably go sometime next Monday, Tuesday, or so." As if it made little difference.

"Monday or Tuesday my foot!" I bellowed. "Either you find out if there is a church near your campsite, or you don't go. Didn't you know that it is a serious sin — a mortal sin — to intentionally miss Mass on Sunday?" I asked.

Tim did not know. Here was my son, after twelve years of Catholic schooling, who thought the notion of attending Mass on Sunday was a "family rule" and not one laid down by God or the Catholic Church. Tim said he never heard of the precepts (that is, the commandments) of the Church and did not realize that "to assist at Mass on all Sundays and holy days of obligation" meant exactly that — it was an *obligation*, a requirement, not an option.

Now it was our turn. The lesson we learned from Tim was, "Never assume!" In spite of the fact that all of our thirteen children attended either Catholic elementary and secondary schools or CCD classes, we no longer assume they will receive or *remember* all of the precepts of our faith.

The Church teaches that the education that parents owe their children is far more than an academic one, or a preparation for economic security. As the *Declaration on Christian Education* of the Second Vatican Council exhorts us, we must try to educate our children "in virtue, to guide them toward a mature freedom and responsibility, and to assist them to grow in faith, hope, and love."

When our son Tony was eighteen, he was always asking about rules and regulations, whether in the family, the school, or life in general. He was also the one whose zest for enjoying the "fullness of life" would test those bounds to the limits.

Once, when he was referring to a holy day of obligation, Tony said, "I thought we had some sort of commandments of the Church."

When I responded "We do," he immediately began to tell me about the talk he had with his boss who "calls himself a Catholic but says he doesn't believe that we are obligated to attend Mass on holy days. He also doesn't believe in the authority of the Pope, or in the Church's position on contraception, divorce, homosexuality, or abortion." Hmmm.

"Does he believe in Jesus?" I couldn't resist asking.

"Yeah. But he says we don't have to believe in everything in order to belong to the Church," Tony responded.

"Well, I'm sure your boss is sincere," I said. "And I think you should be polite in your discussions with him, remembering not to judge or become argumentative. He obviously believes that what he's saying is okay. But it's not."

Ultimately, God is the judge, and I believe he will be more merciful with people like Tony's boss (who obviously has never been properly taught Church teaching) than he will toward those who were told the truth, know the truth, and *then* choose to reject it and do it "their way."

"You know the truth, Tony. And God — *and we* — expect you to live it."

The precepts of the Church are there to protect the faith and to help bring us closer to God. We must remember that the Church was given this authority by Christ himself, who appointed Peter as the head, when our Lord said: "And I tell you, you are Peter, and on this rock I will build my church, and the gates of Hades will not prevail against it. I will give you the keys of the kingdom of heaven, and whatever you bind on earth will be bound in heaven, and whatever you loose on earth will be loosed in heaven" (Matthew 16:18-19).

Every time we say the Nicene Creed, which is recited as part of the Mass each Sunday, we are stating our beliefs in the Catholic Church and her authority.

A helpful and handy resource our family has come to know and rely on is a catechism. (I myself used several editions in preparing certain parts of the manuscript for this book.) Every Catholic home should have one. I can't count the number of times it has supplied the answers we've needed!

I remember the time my Chrissy came home from school and said her high-school teacher announced the birth of his baby and then added that he and his wife might "postpone the baptism until the child is either 'ready' or old enough to select his own religion." This wouldn't be shocking except for the fact that this occurred in a Catholic high school and the teacher was Chrissy's *religion* teacher.

Before I got any hotter under the collar, Chrissy was already headed for the catechism. She read the section on the "parents' obligation to baptize their young," and packed it in her schoolbag for the next morning's class. The following day she returned home to report that *several* students in her class not only challenged the teacher's theology but at least one other classmate quoted from a catechism.

This unfortunate experience was a lesson in faith not just to Chrissy but to John and me — and hopefully her religion teacher! I was glad for the presence of a catechism so it would not appear that we were personally attacking or picking on Chrissy's instructor. Sad to say, the young man had truly been misinformed in this area.

Catholics believe that Christ clearly established the authority of the Pope as well as that of bishops and priests. Yet in a very real sense we, as lay people and members of Christ's Church, are called upon to act as leaders and prophets. Father Mark Dosh, former philosophy and theology professor at St. Paul Seminary, tells his suburban parishioners: "Catholics act in a prophetic way every time they speak of the unconditional love that God has for all members of their family, and then their children see them making that love visible for the neighbor who is hungry, thirsty, naked, sick, or in prison. They speak as prophets when they strive to fulfill just laws in a patriotic spirit so that, when they argue against unjust laws (such as abortion), their words correspond to their previous doing of justice."

It is up to us, then, to live the faith visibly and to expect our young — from tot to teen to young adult — to do the same. We must be obedient to God's laws and the commandments of the Church. If we are wishy-washy or noncommittal, so also will our kids be.

And what are the chief precepts, or commandments, of the Church?

1 ● TO ASSIST AT MASS ON ALL SUNDAYS AND HOLY DAYS OF OBLIGATION. This precept is based on the Third Commandment of God, which requires believers to "keep holy the Sabbath day." Therefore, the Church teaches that if a Catholic intentionally misses Mass on Sunday or a holy day of obligation (without good reason, that is, sickness or unavailability because of work or distance), it is a mortal sin. Holy days were instituted by the Church to remind us of the mysteries of our faith and of the important events in the lives of Christ and of his Blessed Mother and the saints.

2 ● TO FAST AND TO ABSTAIN ON THE DAYS APPOINTED. All baptized persons between the ages of twenty-one and fifty-nine are obliged to observe the fast days of the Church (to eat only one full meal, with two lesser portioned meals, and no snacking in between) unless they are excused or dispensed.

All Catholics who have passed their fourteenth birthday are required to abstain from meat on designated days by the Church. Days of fast and abstinence are established to help us learn self-control; as a means of offering penance for our sins; and to turn our attention, giving honor and glory to God.

3 ● TO CONFESS OUR SINS AT LEAST ONCE A YEAR. Because the Church believes we need the help of frequent confession, we are obliged to confess our sins to a priest at least once a year if we are aware of mortal sin on our soul. Frequent confession keeps us in the state of grace and helps us become more virtuous and to withstand temptations that come to us.

4 ● TO RECEIVE HOLY COMMUNION AT LEAST ONCE A YEAR. The Easter duty requiring one to receive Communion at least once annually begins on the first Sunday of Lent and ends on Trinity Sunday. A Catholic who, knowing this obligation, willfully neglects to receive Holy Communion worthily during this time, commits a mortal sin. Holy Communion is food for the soul. We are literally starving ourselves spiritually if we neglect to receive this sacrament frequently.

5 ● TO CONTRIBUTE TO THE SUPPORT OF THE CHURCH. Every Catholic is obliged to help alleviate the financial burden of the Holy See, the diocese, and the parish.

6 ● TO OBSERVE THE LAWS OF THE CHURCH CONCERNING MARRIAGE. The Church honors the married vocation, and recognizes marriage to be a sacramental sign of Christ's love for his bride, the Church. Christian husbands and wives are visible sacramental signs of our Lord's love and they are to be witnesses to others of God's love. All love comes from God and should lead back to him.

The Church as a family of faith has the duty to assist married people in problems that threaten their marriages. Before a marriage the priest who is to assist at the marriage has the responsibility to see that the couple are free to marry, that they receive sufficient instruction to realize the importance and dignity of the sacrament they are about to receive, and that they are aware of the purposes and the meaning of marriage, and are entering into a genuine marriage covenant.

To assist in providing such pastoral care, Church law insists that unless a dispensation is given, a Catholic can be married validly *only* in the presence of a priest and witnesses.

While the Church can never permit divorce and remarriage, it does, when there are grave reasons for this, permit the separation of partners. Moreover, the Church may at times judge that an apparent marriage was never a true marriage, that no real covenant was established (for example, if one of the partners failed to give, or was incapable of giving, free consent; or if one or both did not intend a real marriage, a permanent bond of faithful love, and an openness to offspring). If for any reason an apparent marriage was not a genuine marriage from the start, it may be possible to obtain an annulment from the Church.

A Catholic who is a partner in an invalid marriage — that is, marriage outside the Church; marriage to a close relative; marriage in which one or both of the partners has been validly married before — is in reality and before God not married to his or her apparent spouse. Hence the performance of the marriage act within that union, although it may be valid in the eyes of the law, is *not* a sacred and holy seal of married love but *really* a wrongful use of sex. Those who have seriously disobeyed divine or ecclesiastical law by entering into an invalid marriage have a duty to return to the state of grace as quickly as possible, and certainly to abstain from Holy Communion until they do. Some solution is always possible even in the most difficult cases.

Angela Kuharski Age 11
B
Saint Joseph Edition
the new
american
Bible
bible

21

❧

Soaking Up Scripture

A complaint often heard from parents of small children is, "It's so hard to find the time during the day to pray." Speaking for myself, my days were much harder when I *didn't* take the time to pray! In fact, prayer and Scripture reading have become invaluable to me.

Like many other Christians who strive to make prayer and reflection part of their daily lives, I once tried to chart a specific formula and neatly plan my schedule to make it happen. But now, as the busy mother of thirteen children, I must be honest and admit that I've long abandoned all hope of set formulas and rigid schedules.

Nevertheless, without prayer and reliance on the word of God, my day would be one long struggle and a series of repetitive homemaking tasks. But my prayer life is done more by "plot" than by plan. I've learned that a busy woman's most basic strategy is to make the most of opportunities that come her way. I watch for the "lulls" rather than the leisure. I secretly sandwich my Scripture between school bells, curfews, and runs to the store for peanut butter and jelly.

I begin my day with the Morning Offering. This I *try* to do before my toes touch the bedroom floor because I know that once I reach for the baby, begin changing diapers, start making breakfasts, doing laundry, or answering the phone, it becomes harder and harder to pray. Offering up each and every prayer, work, joy, and suffering to the Sacred Heart of Jesus gives me purpose and meaning for the day's activities — come what may!

Because of my heavy involvement as a pro-life activist and speaker, I look forward to reading the newspaper and other periodicals that help keep me up on the world outside of Pahl Avenue. One of my cardinal rules, however, is that I never allow myself to read *anything* until I have finished my morning prayers and readings. This little rule is but one small reminder that *Christ comes before everyone and everything.*

I live just one block from church, and on most days — if there is no major crisis and I can make it over the spilled cereal and past my bantering bunch of early risers — I attend the eight o'clock morning Mass. "God is so merciful — he knows who to keep a close eye on," I often tell my friends. What a blessing to have the Eucharist a block away. And what a source of grace to carry me through my day's work!

I often feel as if Christ literally leaps out of the Scripture readings at Mass as I find personal application and significance to the circumstances of my own life. It's gratifying to know that these same readings are being proclaimed at Masses in unison with the Body of Christ all over the world.

On the feast days that commemorate a special saint, I often find other kinds of blessings. For example, on the feast of the apostle St. James the Greater, I offer my Mass intentions particularly for my younger brother Jim, whom I'm not able to see very often.

It's an added source of support and strength for me to remember that all of the great saints and heroes of the Church encountered their own trials and tribulations. When I hear some of their stories at daily Mass, I'm reminded that it was the endurance of those very trials and sufferings for Christ's sake that truly made them saints.

I'm one of those type A personalities that "always has about three things going at once," as my mild-mannered husband, John, likes to describe me. Quite honestly, it took years of a frantic I-wish-I-had-more-time-to-pray existence before I realized that if I wasn't praying it was *my fault*, not God's. My priorities were out of kilter and I appeased my conscience by saying I was too busy serving God.

When I did begin to read the Bible on a steady basis, it wasn't long before the story of Mary and Martha convicted me: I must never busy myself so much, or allow myself to become so "anxious and upset" (as Jesus described Martha), that I fail to trust that God is in control. This is a lesson I learn and relearn almost daily.

Sad to say, motherhood and most especially the influence and importance of the stay-at-home mother have been denounced and denigrated by an antilife, career-oriented, "me-first" culture.

Yet we Christians know — and our faith confirms — that women truly are the "heart" of the home and that each one of us is uniquely called by God to fulfill a specific mission on earth.

A daily devotion to the Scriptures has helped me become aware of my own valuable vocation as a wife, mother, and full-time homemaker. I am often reminded that Christ stayed at Mary's and Joseph's side until he was thirty years of age. What nurturing by Mary and guidance by Joseph must our Lord have drawn upon before he began his public ministry!

The Scriptures also remind me of the uniqueness of being a woman. It is women who are so keenly attuned to the feelings, joys, frustrations, fears, and futures of their loved ones. And it is we who have the responsibility bestowed by our nature and vocation to nurture and to nourish our impressionable children — in addition to other vulnerable family members in need of our care.

The more I read the Scriptures, the greater my devotion to the Blessed Mother. Mary was a beacon of trust: Imagine her confusion and fear when she and Joseph brought their infant Son to the temple for the circumcision ceremony and were told by the prophet Simeon, "This child is destined for the falling and the rising of many in Israel, and to be a sign that will be opposed so that the inner thoughts of many will be revealed — and a sword will pierce your own soul too" (Luke 2:34-35)! Yet her faith never wavered. I pray for the grace to have that kind of trust.

Mary had courage: She was present throughout Christ's public ministry and witnessed the occasions when her precious son was nearly stoned and forced to flee for his life. In the end, she was there with the weeping women as she saw Jesus being led to his death on the cross. She never abandoned her Son. I pray for that kind of courage and faith.

In small ways, we Christian mothers often have to bite our tongues or wait and pray as we watch our children — young and old — go through the challenges of life.

In another vein, the Bible tells us of many courageous

women. Moses' mother, for instance, was willing to give up her son in order to avoid his being killed by the Egyptians and in the hope that he would subsequently be adopted and nurtured by another. She put her infant son in a basket and placed him in the reeds on the riverbank, where he was found and raised by Pharaoh's daughter. Talk about unselfish love! Then there is the story of Elizabeth, our Blessed Mother's older cousin and mother to one of the Church's greatest saints, John the Baptist. She was truly a woman of faith and hope. And let's not forget Abraham's wife, Sarah, who was advanced in years, yet never doubted God's word that she would give birth to Isaac.

As a mom to many, I've given birth to babies in my 20s, in my 30s, and, yes, in my 40s. It's nice to know of some biblical women who also "bucked the system" and had children in the later years of their lives.

The Bible continually reminds me that God knew and planned each and every one of us. To God, the Divine Creator, there is no "unplanned," "unwanted," imperfect baby. "For it was you [O Divine Creator,] who formed my inward parts; you knit me together in my mother's womb" (Psalm 139:13). As an adopted child myself, and mother to six adopted children, it is no small consolation to know that God saw each one of us as a plan and a promise.

The story of Ruth in the Old Testament, which describes her loyalty and love for her mother-in-law, was truly an inspiration to me and brings to mind John's mother who, until her death in 1989, lived just up the street from us.

When I was a young mother, she helped baby-sit, sent over her famous homemade applesauce or rhubarb dessert, and offered her opinion (whether I wanted it or not) on almost everything. As the years went by, it was I who began to look after her, to send over special meals, see to it that her yard work and heavy tasks were done, and to offer *my* opinion (unwelcome as it was) when I felt she needed medical care or attention. Through it all, I grew to love and admire her tremendously. What a privilege it was to have this dear lady in our lives and what a void she left ever since she slipped from our presence.

Feeling the increasing desire for a more regimented daily

prayer life, I felt drawn to join the Third Order Carmelites as a way to strengthen and focus my prayer life. "Third Orders" provide a way for laypersons (both single and married) to express and live out a radical Christian commitment in their secular walks of life. As a lay Carmelite, I have promised to live out my vocation as a wife, homemaker, and mother in obedience to God's will. As part of my Carmelite vow, I attend Mass, pray the Rosary, and read the "Little Office," which is prayed at approximately seven intervals throughout the day, with Scripture readings as its main source.

My commitment as a member of the Third Order Carmelites has not only brought me closer to Christ and the Church but has made the word of God even more alive in my everyday work. I must say, however, that the closer I grow to God, the more I realize how truly weak and fragile is my faith life. Yet God's forgiveness and love knows no limits. In essence, he wants us *all* to be saints!

I admit that, unlike the picture of the serene nun kneeling in solitude before the Blessed Sacrament, I'm more often kneeling over a scrubbed floor, slipping my Scripture sessions between laundry and lunch, or sitting in the waiting rooms of dentists' or doctors' offices. It's then as they come to me that I take the opportunities to pray, reflect, and read Scripture. I know from experience that each opportunity is one that makes God present, active, and *first* in my "type-A three things at once" day!

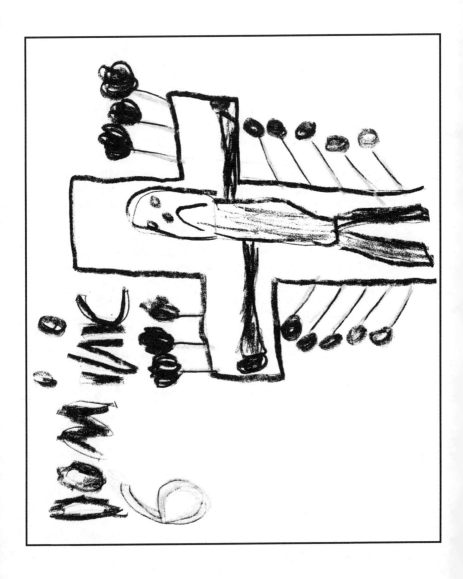

22

❦

Promoting Chastity and Values

Kids have a wonderful sense of knowing who really cares and believes in them. If an influential adult sets a high standard of behavior for a young person, the child will strive to live up to it. Young people like to prove themselves and earn the respect of others — especially someone they look up to.

Think about your own teen years. If you felt like I did, temptation was *everywhere*! So what kept you from being promiscuous but instead helped you stay relatively on the straight and narrow? The usual response is, "Because my parents would've killed me."

On the contrary, the real answer is because we didn't want to disappoint our parents and family. There was a certain amount of love and expectation there, and it was important enough to maintain, even during those tumultuous teen years. Now it's up to us to love our kids enough to expect the same standards of behavior from them.

Even outsiders can convey genuine love, respect, and support to youngsters within their sphere of influence. For instance, I had a godmother who called me periodically to see if I was behaving. Our conversations were fun and light. I *knew* she was genuinely interested in me. In fact, I enjoyed it when she asked me about my "latest flame" (or "flames" as the case may have been at the time). She let me know that, besides my parents, she was one of many people who loved me and expected great things of me.

My pastor, Father Frank Kittock, is an outstanding example of a role model and mentor. His parting words to his graduating eighth graders are caring and warm. He interviews each one privately and, in the course of the conversation, asks the individual if he or she is going to Mass regularly on Sunday.

When he comes across one or two who say they don't go because their "parents don't," he responds firmly but with love: "That's no excuse. You're old enough to go to Mass on your own. I know you can do it and I want you to know that I'll be watching for you from now on." Imagine the young people who are practicing Catholics today because they knew Father Kittock believed in them and cared about them!

Sad to say, the skyrocketing teenage pregnancy and abortion rate as well as the increase in shoplifting and other crimes, violence, and various forms of perversion committed by today's restless young may be more than partially blamed on the parents and influential adults who quit believing and offered these youth little in the way of spiritual and moral principles.

There are five essential "ingredients" necessary in promoting chastity to children. If Christian parents follow this "recipe" during a child's growing-up years it will lessen, if not diminish entirely, the chance that outside influences will permanently undermine a youngster's morals.

Key phrases our children need to hear often:

1 ● "I LOVE YOU!" Never assume that they already know.

2 ● "I BELIEVE IN YOU!" It may not always be easy to make this statement, but you can do it.

3 ● "HOW ABOUT A HUG?" A reassuring reminder and visible sign of support and love.

4 ● "I'M PRAYING FOR YOU!"

5 ● "WITH GOD'S HELP YOU CAN DO GREAT THINGS!"

Mary Lee's story is an example of a life turned around because of the memory of a close relative's influence.

She was raised Catholic, yet in her teen years life became very difficult. Her mother died of cancer when she was eighteen. Her brother died in a car accident the following year. Shortly after, her father remarried, leaving Mary Lee alone and with more independence than she could handle. She was hurting and lonely!

Unfortunately, Mary Lee found companionship in an older married man who was also her employer. Soon she was pregnant and feeling even more isolated. Not only did the news of her pregnancy threaten her reputation, it meant her job!

Why didn't Mary Lee get an abortion? Because she recalled what her grandmother had told her years earlier when "she had taken me aside and talked to me about abortion and what an evil thing it was. It would have broken Grandma's heart if she ever thought I had an abortion."

So here was a grandmother who never saw the grandchild she saved from abortion; but, nonetheless, it was her influence that helped give that little one the gift of life.

After making adoption plans for her baby, Mary Lee became an active volunteer with a pro-life agency working with other women who face a crisis pregnancy.

We can be that same positive influence to the young people in our lives if we only take the time to care. Kids are hungry for strong values to live by.

I still remember the day I was speaking in a large suburban high school as the "pro-life response" to the Planned Parenthood speaker who had been there the day previously and openly advocated contraceptives and abortion.

As I finished showing the slides on abortion, a big football-type fellow shouted across the room, "When is someone going to come here and talk to us about how to say 'no' instead of talking to us after it's too late?"

When indeed? The young man is a reminder of how much society fails its young when they are offered education devoid of values and treated like animals.

Kids want *clear* guidelines and rules, and my son Charlie is a good example. When he was a junior at a Catholic high school, he came home one day complaining about his religion teacher. "He's supposed to tell us right from wrong. We're not the teachers. We're the students," Charlie protested.

"Today Bob asked Mr. A in class if premarital sex was a sin, and Mr. A said, 'Well, Bob, never mind what I think. It really depends on what *you* think.' That guy is so wishy-washy. We never get a straight answer out of him. All he talks about is 'choices' and forming our own conscience."

Before I could say anything, Charlie's next line summed it

up: "What do I care what Bob thinks about sex before marriage? I don't even care what Mr. A or anyone in that class thinks. I just want to know what I'm supposed to think. This doesn't mean I'm always going to do it. But at least I'll know what I'm *supposed* to think."

And rightly so. Kids *can't form a conscience* if they have nothing to form it around.

Our children need to know the truth and should be aware of the following:

● Sex outside of marriage — including petting, sexual "experimentation," homosexual practices, fornication, and adultery — are serious sins and violations of God's Sixth Commandment.

● There is no contraceptive, no pill, no spray or device that can *guarantee* protection against herpes, venereal disease, or the deadly AIDS virus.

● Living chaste and pure lives and saving the gift of their sexuality for marriage is possible, attainable, and beautiful. In fact, a majority of Americans, people of all faiths, still believe this is how God wants us to live our lives.

● Even more, our young people deserve to know that sex outside of marriage robs them of something special. It cheats them of their self-respect and an inner peace and happiness that no sexual encounter can equal.

For our kids' sakes, their health, their self-image, their very lives, we must never give a double message. We must never say, "Don't. But if you do. . ." Ask any teen. They *know* those words mean permission.

We would never offer a double message on abusive eating habits, smoking, alcohol or chemical abuse, and we can't waver when it comes to promoting chastity. Our children's lives and very souls are at stake.

Unfortunately, most educators in government-sponsored schools have done just that by teaching "safe-sex" practices, with contraceptives and abortion as a backup, showing little regard for the fact that sex outside of marriage will profoundly affect a child's emotional, physical, and spiritual well-being — forever.

Christian parents cannot lose faith. God assures us we have more power and influence than *any* outsider and he will give us the grace necessary to fulfill our role. This is an area that cannot be left to others, even if the sex education is offered in a Christian school setting. Remember, we parents are the *primary educators of our young*, and God will hold us accountable if we abdicate our role.

I remember the time I received a notice that my daughter Theresa would be viewing a film on AIDS. Parents were invited to come to the school to preview the material first because of the "sensitive subject matter."

Now let me just say that I'm not known as a "room mom" by my kids' schools. They don't see much of me, and my involvement in PTA and extracurricular events borders on "shameful." I excuse myself by blaming it on "so much to do."

Yet when I went to Theresa's school to view the "controversial film," I was the *only* parent who came. The teacher apologetically reported that one other parent called and said she wanted to come but didn't know if she could fit it into her schedule. I can now truly understand why educators begin to *assume* the parents' responsibility of approving or disapproving school-related activities such as the showing of AIDS films.

As children pass from adolescence to the teen years and ultimately young adulthood, many temptations and challenges will face them. All the more reason we need to be clear and consistent, occasionally repeating or reminding them of how God calls them to live. It's not always easy, especially for those over-eighteen youngsters still living at home.

My theme is, "As long as you're living under our roof, your behavior and lifestyle must not be scandalous or sinful." And yet we, like most parents, are occasionally tested and challenged.

I remember the time one of my daughters innocently asked "if it would be all right" for her and a girlfriend to go camping for the weekend with their boyfriends. All four truly were good kids and saw nothing wrong with the trip because, after all, they would be "sleeping in different tents." I told her as distinctly as I could that it would be "over my dead body," then tried to carefully explain why.

Another daughter, a real sun "freak," thought I grew up

with "turn of the century" (nineteenth, not twentieth) principles because I refused to allow her to wear a two-piece bathing suit. Most of those things are little more than two shoestrings holding a couple of coasters over strategic spots — "X-rated" *even* in my backyard!

On another occasion, one of my grown sons (then twenty-one) couldn't believe we would object to his and a buddy's "saving motel expenses" by rooming with their dates ("separate beds," of course), when they traveled overnight for a friend's wedding.

"You can't do that. It's an occasion of sin." I said. His face fell. My kids think I make these rules up as I go along.

"We're all adults and close friends," he countered. "You know me better than that. I think too much of this girl to do anything out of line," he innocently insisted.

"Well, if sleeping in the same room with your girlfriend doesn't light your torch, then I wanna take you in for testing to make sure you're all there," I replied.

That evening, John and I explained to him that it was more than an occasion of sin. It would cause scandal to the girl, to him, and to those who view them as Catholics living in a secular world. The bottom line: He could not do such a thing while living under our roof. We asked for his word and he gave it.

Quite often, a young person is really innocent of wrongdoing. Lack of experience, lack of time to contemplate the consequences, or pure naïveté can wreak havoc on the young. That's what parenting is all about. And it's up to us, even if our "popularity" temporarily slips, to tell them.

God commands us to stand firm and remind our young:

✔ **Avoid all "occasions of sin."** This may include people, places, or things. Automatic "nos" are situations that involve excessive drinking, chemical abuse, and provocative talk, dress, or actions. (Staying overnight with a person of the opposite gender *is* provocative.)

✔ **Actions can cause scandal to others or lead them to commit sin**. "Tell me how many of your friends will really believe *nothing will happen?*" we asked our daughter and son during the "overnight" arguments. In each case, they had no answer because in their hearts they *knew* that most of their acquaintances would *assume* they were sexually involved.

"Even if you don't do anything wrong," we told our young, "you are known as *Christians* and your actions will cause scandal to others and set bad example."

✔ **Would you approve of the same behavior if you thought Dad and I (or someone else you respect) did the same thing?**

✔ **As parents we have a moral obligation and we will ultimately have to answer to God if we neglect or condone sinful behavior.** I have enough sins of my own without adding any more to the batch!

I firmly believe that we by our actions — perhaps more than our words — will have the greatest impact on our children's behavior. In teaching them chastity, however, we must never *presume* or leave it up to others. Tell them how you feel and why. Don't assume they know or presume they will remember without occasional reminders.

Find a comfortable time when the talk can be free and unrushed. I like to start out when they're young and give it to them in small doses. Anything wordy or preachy, *I've learned*, gets lost.

Sometimes, I lead in by asking them to read a short article or pamphlet, or talk about someone they know, framing it around what God asks of us. Forgiveness and God's mercy should always be apparent to our young.

Our message on chastity:

✔ **We believe in you!** God and we expect you to save the gift of your sexuality for marriage. It takes tremendous willpower, self-control, but we know you can do it.

✔ **You are a gift, and so is your sexuality.** You were created in the image and likeness of God. He has a plan and a purpose just for you, and your sexuality is a very intimate and intricate part of that plan.

The act of sexual intercourse was designed by God to be a gift of life and love. It is so profound, so powerful, and so beautiful because it has the potential to do two things: (1) To express love between a husband and wife. (2) To transmit new life — bringing a new baby into the world.

To use sex outside of marriage, whether for personal satisfaction or even when meant as a symbol of love, is to cheapen or abuse God's gift, and is a serious sin.

✔ **Beware of those who don't believe in you.** They treat the sexual urge as if it's little more than an "appetite," reducing you to the level of an animal. Don't listen to them.

You'll never feel good about yourself or treat others with the respect they deserve if you follow your "feelings" rather than God's laws and the high standards that will guarantee you real happiness and love. You can bet you're going to be tempted, but we know you are strong. You can do it.

✔ **There's no such thing as "safe sex" outside of marriage.** Every sexual act is open to the possibility of pregnancy.

When it's outside of marriage, you are also exposing yourself and your mate to the possibility of disappointment, disease, and even death. Venereal disease can cause feelings of guilt, shame, and sterility. There is no known cure for AIDS and it can result in death. Don't be selfish and sorry. It's worth the wait!

Don't be fooled. God's laws still apply today: Sex outside of marriage is dangerous and sinful! Save the gift of you and your sexuality for marriage the way God intends you to do. We have faith in you!

✔ **Promise yourself that you will stay away from anything that will weaken your resistance or destroy the gift of your sexuality.** Stay away from illegal drugs, alcohol, or mood-altering chemicals of any kind. They are addictive, dangerous, and will damage your reputation as well as weaken your resistance to evil.

✔ **Think of the kind of spouse you would like to marry. Promise to save yourself for that someone special.** Save your affection and passion for someone you truly love. Real love doesn't have to prove it. Real love is willing to sacrifice. Real love shows self-control and can wait — for the good and well-being of both partners.

✔ **It's never too late for chastity!** Virginity means "never having had sexual intercourse." Chastity means purity, that is, to decide to abstain from unlawful (outside of marriage) sex.

Premarital intercourse, petting (touching forbidden or

genital areas), and sexual experimentation are all sinful. If you've been sexually involved, stop now. Ask for God's forgiveness and the grace to help you stay on course.

Remember, no matter the past, it's never too late to get back your self-control and resume practicing the virtue of chastity. The temptations won't disappear, but once you make that pledge to save yourself for marriage, you'll experience an inner peace and joy that cannot be matched.

✔ **Keep your dates light,** travel with others, and double-date whenever possible. It offers a safety net to runaway emotions.

✔ **Remember that the majority of teens are virgins and want to be.** Don't be fooled into believing that "everyone is doing it." Not true.

✔ **Teens have tremendous self-control and discipline.** All we need do is look at the accomplishments made by young people, whether it's the Olympics, Peace Corps, 4-H, Guardian Angels, Scouts, sports, music, or in the area of academics to see self-sacrifice and self-control at their best!

✔ **Stay close to God and those who love and believe in you — your family.** God will give you all the grace you need to say "no" to sin. No temptation is more powerful than our Lord's love and grace. Don't let anyone sell you short or rob you of the gift of your sexuality. We're your parents and we believe in you.

A Final Word

I hope this little book has been of help to you in one way or another — especially if you are just starting a family. This is not meant to be a "how to raise your family" guide; rather, it is designed to encourage you to rely a lot on God, on prayer, on asking that God's will be done on a daily basis. If it helps you to pray just a little bit more, then say with me: "Praise the Lord!"

Bibliography

The Catholic Catechism, Bishop Donald W. Wuerl, Thomas Comerford Lawler, and Ronald Lawler, O.F.M., Cap. (Huntington, Ind.: Our Sunday Visitor, Inc., 1986).

Covenant of Love: Pope John Paul II on Sexuality, Marriage and Family in the Modern World, Rev. Richard M. Hogan and Rev. John M. LeVoir (Garden City, N.Y.: Doubleday & Co., Inc., 1985).

Declaration on Christian Education, Gravissimum Educationis [NCWC (now the NCCB and USCC) trans., 1965], Daughters of St. Paul (Boston: Saint Paul Books & Media, n.d.).

Dogmatic Constitution on the Church, Lumen Gentium [NCWC trans. based on *L'Osservatore Romano*, Nov. 25, 1964], Daughters of St. Paul (Boston: Saint Paul Books & Media, n.d.).

I Believe in Love: Retreat Conferences on the Interior Life, Père Jean de Coeur de Jesus D'Elbeé, tr. Marilyn Teichert with Madelein Stebbins (Paris: Éditions Saint-Michel, 1969; Chicago: Franciscan Herald Press, 1974).

Mother Teresa, the Early Years, David Porter (Grand Rapids, Mich.: Eerdmans Publishing Co., 1986).

Orphans of War: Work with the Abandoned Children of Vietnam, 1967-1975, Rosemary Taylor (London: Collins Publishing, 1988).

Parent Power: A Common Sense Approach to Raising Children in the 80's, Dr. John K. Rosemond (Charlotte, N.C.: Eastwood Press, 1981).

Pastoral Constitution on the Church in the Modern World, Gaudium et Spes [NCWC trans., 1965] Daughters of St. Paul (Boston: Saint Paul Books & Media, n.d.).

St. Joseph Baltimore Catechism (Official Revised Edition), explained by Rev. Bennet Kelley, C.P. (New York: Catholic Publishing Book Co., n.d.).

Saint of the Day, Vol. 2, ed. Leonard Foley, O.F.M. (Cincinnati, Ohio: St. Anthony Messenger Press, 1975).

Six-Point Plan for Raising Happy, Healthy Children, Dr.

John K. Rosemond (Kansas City, Mo.: Andrews & McMeel, 1989).

The Teaching of Christ: A Catholic Catechism for Adults (Abridged Edition), ed. Ronald Lawler, O.F.M., Cap., Donald W. Wuerl, and Thomas Comerford Lawler (Huntington, Ind.: Our Sunday Visitor, Inc., 1979).

The World's First Love, Bishop Fulton J. Sheen (New York: McGraw-Hill, Inc., 1952).